IT'S TIME
YOUR
AWESOME LIFE
AWAITS

ROB VIVIAN

ISBN: 978-1-77374-066-9 (Print)
ISBN: 978-1-77374-067-6 (Ebook)

Typeset and cover design by Edge of Water Designs, edgeofwater.com

OTHER BOOKS BY THE AUTHOR

The Grass is Greener on This Side of the Fence

The Realtor's Magic Formula

Success Explosion

Expecting Awesome Daily

ACKNOWLEDGEMENTS

Being in a position to author several books would not be possible without the important people in my life who supply me with an amazing support system. It really is difficult to mention everyone, as many have positively influenced me physically, mentally, and spiritually.

My parents, Fran and Norm, have had the greatest influence on my life. Over the years they have taught me a wide range of skills, including what to do and at times what not to do.

As I often mention, I am prone to mentally wander. Colleen, my wife of almost 37 years—obviously she is very patient!—is there to keep me grounded, for which I am thankful.

My children, Josh and Corissa, are amazing and play significant roles in the daily operation of my company, Rob Vivian Coaching. They make an amazing duo in the office.

My siblings Norma, Randy, Rick, and Eric have and have always had my back; I appreciate that more than they are aware.

Last, but certainly not least, I thank God for my life of blessings: I definitely don't deserve it, but I'll take it!

Something Awesome Is Going To Happen Today!

IT'S TIME
YOUR
AWESOME LIFE
AWAITS

ROB VIVIAN

TABLE OF CONTENTS

Acknowledgements v

For Starters... xiii

Chapter One: What Your Life Should Be...................................... 1

Chapter Two: It's Never Too Late 11

Chapter Three: Rain is Required 19

Chapter Four: Allow the Past to Influence, Not Control 27

Chapter Five: Slow Down 35

Chapter Six: Do What You Know is Right 43

Chapter Seven: The Joy is in the Now 53

Chapter Eight: Reflect a Lot.. 61

Chapter Nine : Embrace Generosity 71

Chapter Ten: Less Thinking, More Doing.................................. 79

Chapter Eleven: Live Away From the Edge................................ 87

Chapter Twelve: Toughen Up a Bit 105

Chapter Thirteen: Having Money Instead of Money Having You 117

Final Thoughts... 131

About the Author... 133

Notes 135

Do not wait. The time will never be 'just right.

Napoleon Hill

For Starters

WHAT THIS BOOK WILL DO FOR YOU

THE INSPIRATION FOR this book spawns from my many thousands of conversations with everyday people over the phone, during a livestream session, or in-person at a seminar. Individuals are continually pouring out their hearts out to me, sharing their goals and aspirations. I can physically feel emotions well up inside me as they unveil their hearts' desires. Truthfully, it's one of my favourite parts of my job. The energy I feel as they share is real in my heart: a sincere jolt of excitement that is virtually impossible for me to contain. I am overcome by the fact that I will be afforded the opportunity to play a small part in their personal journeys toward their desired successes.

My immediate response is, "When? What's the plan?"

Unfortunately, all too often my enthusiasm is curtailed by their response: "I don't know, but someday."

I become acutely aware that this has been their dream for quite some time, but in many cases little to no action has been taken.

In fact, the only reason it's coming up at all is because there happens to be a presenter in attendance. My logical response is, "Can I ask what you are waiting for?"

This is usually followed by a plethora of (often made-up) reasons that they couldn't possibly achieve this dream now (Hint: these are also commonly referred to as "excuses").

My advice is always, "It's time: your awesome life awaits." In fact, that awesome life is everything they had just shared with me in the past few minutes. It's time to stop talking and start doing: nothing more has to happen. There hasn't been anything in their way; all the stories they have made up are exactly that: stories they made up.

It would be incorrect for me to state that everyone is afflicted with the procrastination bug. My educated best guess would be a 70/30 split: that 70% of people mentally buy into some (usually made-up) reason for why their dreams, goals, and aspirations must be put on hold for the future.

I find it interesting when they share these excuses with me. In my mind, their "reason" for now not being the time to act is actually what makes it the appropriate time. For example, I often hear, "But I'm a little short on finances right now!" Wouldn't that be a great motivator? "But I have small children at home!" Wouldn't this be a perfect opportunity to teach the value of goals, focus and determination?

I could go on, because these reasons (read: excuses) seem endless. When people take the time to make up these excuses, they are effectively casting an obstacle in their own path: they are in their own way. Now is the time.

Not everyone is on the 70% side of the split; I get that. However, it's time to be honest with yourself about which group you are in: are you with the 30% of continual doers or are you one of those 70%

who possesses no shortage of reasons as to why now is not the time. Here's a newsflash: It's time: your awesome life awaits.

I consider myself a strong, committed Christian—which means I don't screw up as much as I did prior to living a life guided by Christian values. Although I am sure God shakes His head in regard to my actions on a regular basis, I'm just doing my best.

I mention this because although my spiritual position is of the utmost importance to me, and I do broach the topic periodically, my writings are not about how to be a spiritual person. My books are about achieving your maximum potential, in both your physical and mental life. I just don't want you to make the mistake of thinking that your position in life is more important than your relationship with your own spiritual values: that would be a grave mistake. One day I may pen a book exploring my thoughts on the subject, but that is not this book (although if you want, I can recommend a good one: the Bible).

The writings in *this* book will explore many different obstacles that we may have inadvertently placed in our paths. It will also cover the ideas and strategies we can implement that will assist us in our endeavours to accomplish the "awesome" that lies in our not-too-distant future.

Specifically, we will take a close look at the following items, from both positive and negative viewpoints: how some concepts hold us back, and how those same concepts can be fuel for our internal engines.

What Your Life Should Be

We each have a path that we should naturally walk; however, it doesn't necessarily mean we are always on that path. I, personally, have been off the path many times; you are probably the same. We will break down this common mistake to get you back on the correct path, as well as to implement strategies that will limit your future waywardness.

It's Never Too Late

I personally love this point, and have relied on its truth many times; in fact, more times than I would care to admit. As long as you breathe air, it's not too late to start acting toward your goals.

Rain is Required

Perspective is everything on this point. If we were a farmer, we would pray for rain periodically. If we lived in a wintery climate, we would hate the rain on our one week of tropical vacation. Rain is required for growth, be it crops or personal improvement. If seas were never rough, sailors would have no need to improve their sailing skills. We mostly don't like the rain, but it is necessary.

Allow the Past to Influence, Not Control

I have heard it said that your past architects your present: that you become what you think about. I don't disagree with that message, I just don't think it's absolute. If your past thoughts and actions completely controlled your present, what would be the point of positive actions and deeds now? You are not held captive by your actions from the past, but it is good to recognize how they influence you.

Slow Down

We live in a fast-paced society, a "right now" mindset. Truth is, that's a very unhealthy way to live. In order to move forward, we must regularly slow down and mentally exhale. It is a vital component to getting to wherever it is you desire to go.

Do What You Know is Right

Success is a very interesting place. It is different for every person, but at the same time it harbours many universal aspects that are, on occasion, difficult to comprehend or define. One of those is doing what is right. We all have our own moral leanings, but a person that continually leans toward what they know to be right will continually be blessed with success. I realize at times it can appear in the short term that this is not the case; however, I can assure you that in the big picture (which is where life takes place), your feelings of success will be influenced by whether you have done what you know to be right.

The Joy Is in the Now

I realize your dreams and aspirations are exciting—mine are too! I also realize that they reside in the future: some may be just about to arrive, while others are further down the path. As awesome as they will be, the joy of life is in the now. Don't take the amazing "now" for granted. Count your blessings daily!

Reflect A Lot

Looking back and taking stock of the past will serve as a very valuable exercise. Those positive events of your past will instil confidence, hope, and direction in your life. Those events that live on the list of poor judgement can also possess value, ensuring we never repeat them. We should consciously make a decision to reflect, and in doing so ensure that at least 90% of those items we reflect on make us feel good or proud.

Embrace Generosity

There are many mandatory success principles, some of which are a little difficult to see the direct cause and effect of. Generosity is one of those. However, we can't really experience a higher level of success without that generous internal spirit. Implementing a sincerely generous mindset will unleash an avalanche of success in your direction.

Less Thinking, More Doing

I don't think our planet has a procrastination problem. I think we have a procrastination epidemic. We would do ourselves a huge favour with a lot less thinking and a lot more doing. Notice I didn't say no thinking: just less. It is better to take the wrong path, and correct yourself along the way, than to remain stuck at the crossroads.

Live Away from the Edge

I realize we live in an increasingly fast-paced society: physically, mentally, and technologically. Life is often a full-contact sport, and occasionally knocks come from all sides. The last thing we need is to take a blow while we are teetering on the edge; the results could catastrophic. Let's move away from the metaphorical danger zone. Better to get knocked down and get back up than to be knocked over the edge.

Toughen Up a Bit

I don't want you to think I am an insensitive person; in fact, those who know me often acknowledge my compassion for others. When I say "toughen up a bit," I'm referring to how our current society seems to feel outraged way too much: that people seem to be far too easily offended. "Toughen up a bit" means more should roll off you, not stick.

Having Money Instead of Money Having You

I have no issue with money; I plan on making a whole bunch more, and I hope you do as well. I just want to have a healthy conversation about money. I want you to have money instead of allowing money to have you. To do so, we need to have way more of these open conversations about money.

I truly want you to have the best life possible, and to that end I will do my very best to fully explain each of these topics and give you tangible items to focus on in order to propel you toward your desired goals. I will also shine a spotlight on those natural traps that could befall you if you are left unawares.

Happy reading!

For every minute you are angry you lose 60 seconds of happiness!

Anonymous

Chapter One

WHAT YOUR LIFE SHOULD BE

THIS CHAPTER WAS initially titled "What your life *could* be." However, as I pondered the scope of that statement, I realized "What your life *should* be" was far more appropriate. There are many things that our lives could be; it's what we believe they *should* be that makes all the difference.

The unfortunate reality is that a minimal number of people achieve their potential: only a small, select group experience what life they should be living. It's unfortunate that the vast majority of people live out their lives at a level that is somewhat less than their potential.

Of course, everyone's life has value, and we all have a considerable contribution to make. But no matter how significant a life may appear, it does not necessarily mean that person has maximized their potential.

I'm not saying in any way that their existence was futile, or that they failed to bring value to themselves and those around them. In fact, after taking stock of their accomplishments, any individual's life would probably be assessed as an absolute success. But this in no way indicates that an individual has achieved their maximum potential, or has experienced everything that life has intended for them.

Like you, I have attended my share of memorials, where friends and family collect positive qualities and funny stories to be shared as a way to process the loss of a loved one. Although I regularly share in the conversation, I can't help but wonder what this individual left on the table: what is it that they intended to do but never got to? Where were they supposed to travel, but never had that experience? Who they were supposed to influence that remained on the bucket list? Most of us pass on from this Earthly life with a sizable number of items unchecked on our to-do list.

The purpose of this book is to jolt you out of procrastination so that you can be all you were intended to be. Your life is probably amazing as it is, and come the time for your celebration of life, there will be many successes, positive qualities, and funny stories to share. However, that is no reason to leave a to-do list behind.

I do a lot of travelling, speaking at various seminars and meeting thousands of incredible people. It's very common for passionate, motivated people to share with me their exciting goals and aspirations, but for those goals to still be on their "someday" list. And I tell them the same thing I am going to tell you: it's time. Make those amazing goals and experiences a reality. You don't want those amazing items to still be on your to-do list when you leave this Earth.

Most people will achieve great things: they may have a satisfying career, raise incredible children, own a comfortable home, have many friends and family to rely upon, or any other exemplary accomplishments. Which is fine for the masses of the world: those that are content with simply "great." However, in the end, some of their stories will go untold simply because they have left them unchecked on a to-do list.

The truth is we are made for so much more. Only a minority of people will deem it important to experience all life has intended for them and go beyond simply "great"—and I want you to be one of them.

Perhaps you feel like you have already completed your to-do list, which is awesome: mission accomplished. However, as you read I think you will realize that life has more in store for you. It's time: your awesome life awaits.

Most people have an ambition to be someone that stands out. In life you are either casting a shadow or living in someone else's. I encourage you to not settle for going quietly unnoticed, spending your days shadowed by another. Cast your own shadow.

In life, we need to frequently ask ourselves, "If not now, then when?" When I hear about people's future dreams and ask them this question, my intention is to challenge them to bring those worthwhile goals from a "future" item to a "now" item.

Yes, in some cases a dream must reside in the future: say, due to other experiences that must come first. However, I can say that in most cases the dreams I hear about can easily exist in the present.

In order to discover what our lives should be, we are required to fully assess what is possible for ourselves in all the aspects of our lives. To do so, we must first consider our "perfect world": if everything went our way, what would each of the aspects of our lives look like? The truth is, very few people invest the time required to develop a clear picture of their perfect future and chart a course to that accomplishment.

Even those that do rarely include all the aspects of their lives in this process. As a business coach, I interact with business people on a daily basis. They have hired me to assist them in taking their business to a new level, and as such their primary goal is increased income. But it never takes long for our new client to discover that the success they seek also includes other, more important, aspects of their lives.

There is a saying that gets applied here: "haste makes waste." First things first, we need to discover what it is that we are trying to achieve. We need a clear mental picture of our destinations; otherwise, we will be like a rudderless boat on a windy day: tossed to and fro at the mercy of the wind. We need to take the time to create a clear picture of the contributions we could make: not only in our own lives, but also in those around us.

The order in which we categorize our priorities is of the utmost importance. We need to ask ourselves some honest questions, and the answers may surprise you.

I teach this principle in my seminars. There, my audience is eager to take their personal business to a much higher level. You can imagine, then, the strange looks I receive when I tell them that money should be the least important part of their lives.

However, I simply ask the group, "In your honest opinion, what is more important to you: money, or your spiritual position?" Most in the group agree that their spiritual position, at least in the big picture, is of greater priority.

"How about your health?" I continue. "What's more important: your money, or your health?" There's 100% agreement on that one: health. "How about your family? Friends?"

Once again, everyone concurs that money takes the second spot. So if money is always second, it must be the least important aspect of your life.

This is our #1 principle that governs success. It sounds crazy, but I don't make up life's crazy sociological systems, I just explain them.

It should be noted that although within your priorities money should correctly be in fifth place, it is also true that money problems do hinder achieving the other four more important aspects. So although it can be a necessity, it is important to keep money in its correct spot at priority position number five. The sooner you can make this adjustment, the faster you will gain ground on your perfect future.

The purpose of this chapter is to discover what our lives should be, and to guard ourselves against leaving a lengthy bucket list behind once we are gone. The first step is to dedicate some thought to what the aspects of our lives should look like.

At the end of this chapter, there will be an exercise designed to assist you in creating exactly that: a clear vision of that perfect you. It's vital that you take the time to connect with what is really important to you, and not what others *think* is important.

To get you brainstorming, I have listed some examples of goals in life's five personal aspects. The intention is not for you to choose items from my breakdown: my thoughts are designed to get you thinking about what ideas you really connect with.

It should also be mentioned that the more specific the better. Casual desires will remain exactly that: casual desires. And I think it's safe to say we have spent enough time in that casual mindset.

Aspects of Your Life:

Spiritual

- Leader in your place of worship
- Leader among your family
- Connecting regularly with your creator
- Being the person others come to in times of crisis
- Possessing a sense of calm and contentment

Familial

- Being the calming force in situations
- Unity and cohesiveness
- Mutual respect
- Unconditional love
- Vibrant, two-way relationships
- Being the patriarch/matriarch

Physical

- Thinking about being healthy versus being skinny
- Body composition
- Holistic healthcare or awareness, such as a naturopath
- Cardio or other good, weekly workouts
- Meeting the daily recommendation for fruits and vegetables

Mental

- Possessing mental calm
- Taking life's natural ebb and flow in stride
- Automatically looking on the bright side
- Finding joy in life's simple things
- Not overly concerned what others think about you

Financial

- Being without money issues that hinder life
- Being generous with your surplus for the correct reasons
- Making wise investments

- Being responsible with resources
- You can be relied upon by family and friends

Again, these ideas are not designed for you to pick from the list: I'm attempting to give you a starting point to assess what is really important to you and what you would like your life to be in the not-too-distant future.

In a Nutshell

The time to add to your amazing journey is today. Procrastination is the chief thief of dreams. Take the necessary time to find out what it is you really want. Recognize that time is of the essence and take the required steps to enhance your journey.

Note that the title for this chapter is what your life "should" be, not "could" be. Until a person can make this switch when thinking about their desired life, they will lack the necessary commitment, passion, and determination to see the process through. Take the time and complete the exercise connected to this chapter and begin your journey.

It's time: your awesome life awaits.

Helpful Exercise

Using the previous pages as a guide, think of the five aspects of your life. What is really important to you? In a perfect world, what would all the aspects of your life (not just a part of your life!) look like? The point of this book is to realize that it's time. First things first, though: time for what?

Spiritual: _____

_____

Familial: _____

_____

Physical: _____

_____

Mental: _____

_____

Financial: _____

_____

Don't be shy. It's your life: be bold, dream big,
you become what you think about!

It always seems impossible until it's done!

Nelson Mandela

Chapter Two

IT'S NEVER TOO LATE

LIFE IS NEVER over until it is over. Therefore, it's never too late to set another worthwhile goal. Until we take our last breath, we should be squarely focused on achieving forward motion toward an honest, worthwhile goal.

In the beginning of our lives, our early years are filled with rudimentary tasks such as learning to walk, speak, and run. We explore the wonders of play and the role that imagination has in our lives when we spend the afternoon as an explorer discovering and conquering new worlds.

Later, we embark on the schooling part of our life journey, in most cases taking up 13 years, and sometimes many more depending on our career path. Although specific facts and knowledge may later appear redundant, the act of learning and advancing in itself presents tremendous value.

As a personal example, I have never had a reason to use algebraic equations if my post education life—for others, pursuing a career involving mathematics, complex algebra may be a common occurrence. On the surface, it would appear that for me, personally, algebra was a waste of precious time. In fact, I would say that opportunities may never present themselves in order for us to implement the vast majority of what we have learned. However, it is the act of learning—and thus growing as people—that has value.

During this portion of your life, there are many things to learn: many opportunities for personal growth and advancement. When those situations arise, the correct thinking is to seize them. It's time: your awesome life awaits.

In the post-education part of your life, you now have a whole new set of decisions that need to be made and an entire set of responsibilities that need your attention. Although the decisions are different, the rules remain constant; when your instincts say it's time, it's time.

I have been teaching this concept for many years, to thousands upon thousands of people. It's very common for people to inquire when the right time to move forward is and when to stay put. My instruction is always the same: when your inner self is clear that this is your path, immediately walk in that direction.

The most common response is, "But what if I make a mistake?" Well then, you would obviously walk back. It's never too late. You probably haven't travelled too far, and you can always backtrack: it's not that big of a deal.

It's been my observation that when most people come to a fork in the road, they set up camp and waste massive amounts of time living at that crossroad. Forks in the road are good things: they prove that you are moving forward. The trick is to assess the situation, make a decision, and—here's the important part—travel in the desired direction.

Will you choose the wrong direction periodically? Of course you will. Turn around, go back, and take the other road. I cannot understate that the fear of an occasional wrong decision does not warrant a lifetime of indecision.

As you travel through your post-education life, forks in the road will show up on a regular basis. Should I spend my life with this person, that person, or is perhaps being single my deal? You might want to spend a bit of time at some of these forks, but at some point a decision is going to be required. Where will I live? What vacation do I want to save for? What lifestyle suits me? The forks just keep coming.

I'm not making light of our life decisions, I'm just pointing out that far too many people spend way too much time at the inevitable forks.

Later on in life, additional forks in the road will expose themselves. For instance, if you have a growing family, should you move to a larger home to accommodate it? Where will the kids continue their post-high school studies? How will you secure yourself financially when retirement presents itself?

Life is full of decisions; these should be welcomed and considered commonplace. Obviously, decisions that must be made vary in importance. Sometimes these forks in the road are significant, while others not so much. Either way the process remains the same: weigh it out, make a decision, and travel vigorously down your chosen path with a positive attitude. If you discover that this path isn't what you expected, simply turn around and go back.

You may have wasted some time or perhaps some resources, but it's never too late. Making decisions is infinitely better than spending your valuable time camping out at the fork: there are better places to camp!

I sometimes think that when we are pre-retirement age, we

somehow spin the idea in our minds that retirement is stationary—that all the forks in the road will have been dealt with. But in reality, that is simply not true. And this is good news! Life will continually bring you to fork after fork, until the day you breathe your last breath.

My spirit rejoices at this good news, and I hope yours does too. If we didn't have to face decisions throughout life, then our later years would resemble being put out to pasture: just sitting around with nothing to do.

I am sure you know some folks who are accomplishing exactly that: sitting around and doing nothing but taking up space. Some of them are likely not even in the older category. The point of this chapter is to make you aware of the fact that life is awesome and exciting, right from the get-go until the very end.

It's never too late to set another goal or dream a new dream. It's true that, depending on where you are in the cycle of life, your goals and dreams will, of course, vary; however, what won't vary is their importance or intensity. As a young person, perhaps you dream about owning your first home. Years of saving will be required in order to achieve that worthwhile goal. It's so amazing when you turn the key in your front door for the first time. Years later, when you attend your child's graduation, the feeling of satisfaction is just as intense.

As you travel throughout life, dreams and goals are accomplished on a regular basis. The goals are different, but the sense of accomplishment is always the same. Down the road, maybe you sell your house in the city and move to a fully-renovated cottage. You sip your morning coffee while looking out at the lake as the morning mist dissipates. There it is again: an amazing sense of satisfaction that wells up from within you.

I sometimes hear people say, "It's too late for me now." But the truth is it's never too late. If you took a wrong turn along the way, turn around and go back. Given the number of forks you will encounter on the road, it is unrealistic to think that you will choose correctly every time. I, personally, have chosen incorrectly many times; there is no shame in cycling back.

For instance, there was a time when I was certain that an entrepreneurial lifestyle was not the correct life for me. Instead, factory life appeared desirable. The confidence of a steady and reliable paycheque seemed like my lot in life.

I spent a few years exploring that pathway, and although that works for most people, clearly this was the wrong path for me. Fortunately, a few years in I recognized my error and quickly made my way back to my starting point. From there, I embarked on my entrepreneurial quest. Some would say I wasted several years of my life; I would say that I would not have been as entrepreneurially committed had I not had that learning experience. Perspective is everything.

Many people have wasted away years settling for something less than their best; however, you can't put toothpaste back in a tube. The great news is today is a new day: today can be your starting point. It's never too late: your awesome life awaits.

At the end of the day, if you have accidently assessed that the decision-making part of your life is over, take a breath and get back in the game. There is a day coming for all of us, where we will no longer be in the game of life; but until then, be an active participant.

It's never too late! The game changes, but it still goes on.

In a Nutshell

Life is a continual, decision-making process from the moment we are born until the day we die. I hope that you find that statement encouraging and, like me, wouldn't want it any other way. Life is full of forks in the road: the excitement of "this way or that way?", the exhilaration of a decision having been made, and the excitement of traveling toward new, unknown experiences waiting just over the horizon. That's the zest of life. Whether you are 10, 40, or 85 years old, it's all the same. It's never too late to set another goal or dream a new dream. It's time: your awesome life awaits.

Helpful Exercise

Let's ask ourselves an honest question. Are we fully involved in this awesome life of ours? Or have we accidently been sitting on the sidelines lately?

It's never too late to set another worthwhile goal or to dream a new dream. Take some time to consider and lay out some goals for yourself for the next 1, 3, and 5 years. It's time!

Something I would like to accomplish within the next year:

_____

_____

_____

Something I would like to accomplish within the next 3 years:

_____

_____

_____

Something I would like to accomplish within the next 5 years:

_____

_____

_____

Question to ask yourself:
If you are not setting goals on a regular basis, what are you doing?

The time for action is now. It's never too late to do something.

Antoine de Saint-Exupery

Chapter Three

RAIN IS REQUIRED

ALTHOUGH WE MIGHT think that experiencing beautiful sunshine every day would be amazing, in reality rain is required.

This principle is easy to see in the literal sense: the Earth needs rain. Trees and plants need it in order to grow and flourish. And although harder to physically see, the concept is just as true on our road to success: we need to experience hardships or face issues in order to grow as a person and succeed.

Sometimes, these issues that arise can feel inconvenient at the very least, or overwhelming at worst. In the moment, it may be difficult to identify a benefit hidden within that current dilemma; however, one probably does exist.

Even though we accept the fact that physical rain is an absolute necessity, we still often find that it falls into the "inconvenient" category. For instance, I personally enjoy cottage life: fishing, swimming, and enjoying a multitude of water sports. There's nothing better than enjoying the lake on a sun-filled day. But some summers only seem to be sunny Monday through Friday and rain every Saturday and Sunday.

In the big picture, I understand that nature needs the rain; I'm just not happy about the inconvenience of it occurring over my weekend. I'm still at the lake cottage, and things are still happening: playing board games, putting a puzzle together, or perhaps watching a movie. As we watch the rain pour down we can say, "Well, the grass needs it," all we want, but we'd still rather it not be happening over that particular weekend. It is a reasonable preference, just not a reasonable request.

In life, metaphorical rain is exactly the same: when it presents itself, from our viewpoint it will appear to be the most inconvenient time. Just like it being sunny all week but pouring on the weekend.

It does happen on occasion when a rainy day presents itself right at the correct moment. In fact, as I write today the skies are open, nourishing the ground. It's a great day for writing. I'm not finding this rainy day inconvenient at all: today fits right into my schedule.

It's true that, on occasion, rain comes at exactly the correct time. However, in most cases rain (both physical and metaphorical) is perceived as having the worst timing. The correct mindset is to purposefully view our rainy event as a necessary component that has been placed on our path to whatever worthwhile destination we have our mind fixed on.

It would be amazing if we could choose the severity of the rains and insert them into our schedule at convenient times; however, I'm sorry to inform you that life doesn't work that way. To wish it otherwise would be to wish you didn't have life; I don't think that is a good idea!

Just like there are multiple severities of rain in the real world, the metaphorical rain of life's setbacks can occur on multiple levels. It can be nothing more than a brief, enjoyable sun shower or something more destructive that forces us to batten down the hatches and hold on for dear life. I suppose it's good that manageable setbacks, like sun showers, are more common than the rain that brings a life-altering scenario.

At the end of the day, rain is unpredictable, mostly inconvenient, and occasionally damaging on many different levels of our being. However, we must accept the fact that rain is a required component to a successfully achieved goal. If the seas were never stormy, a sailor's skills would never improve. Fortunately, seas are occasionally rough, allowing sailors the opportunity for personal growth.

I realize that when you encounter a storm in your life, accepting that it is a necessity may seem like a petty consolation; however, the more we can make that connection, the easier we will find assurance that sunny days are on the horizon.

Although in life the "rain" of challenges is mostly unwanted, there are some hidden benefits. We are given an opportunity to rest, reflect, and overall regroup. We may not appreciate the process, but in the big picture it would be mistake not to acknowledge the benefit of reassessing.

As a literal example, perhaps one rainy day we realize that our roof is no longer doing its job correctly. It may come at an inopportune time financially, but the rain is what makes it clear that an adjustment must be made.

Metaphorical rains by way of problematic situations can also provide the necessary information that allows us to make the proper adjustments. It may not be convenient, but in the big picture it's a blessing that the required adjustment can be made before the situation becomes any worse. Best to patch the roof before the damage is irreparable.

For example, perhaps your doctor informs you that if you continue with your current habits, there will be health problems on your horizon. You now have a choice as to how you can perceive this information. You could process it as an inconvenience: "That's a drag; I can't have my donut every morning now. I love my donut every morning. And who can find the time to exercise? I know I drink a lot, but it takes the edge off my stress."

In this case, I personally think that you should leave the doctor's office on cloud nine. The "rain" of your doctor's bad news has brought some problems to your attention. A series of bad decisions were made, but the "rain" becomes your wake-up call.

So you could consider this rain an inconvenience to your preferred lifestyle, or you can think about the big picture and profusely thank your doctor for his or her honesty. Seen properly, you should welcome this rain. It encourages you to eat better—not perfectly, just better—and embark on an exercise program. You realize that the stress you've been trying to manage by drinking is simply life's normal growing pains when you're stepping out of your comfort zone—and that means you're improving! You are supposed to enjoy that process, not attempt to numb it.

Rain by way of setbacks can also be openly welcomed. For instance, perhaps you are in a relationship that you are acutely aware must end. Delivering the bad news is no one's favorite topic. But instead, your partner is the one to broach the subject, informing you that in their mind, too, the relationship has grown stale. You find a way to part ways and still remain friends. Although a setback in your overall goal in finding a life partner, this period of "rain" gives you a good way to backtrack down your path and pick a new course.

I realize, of course, that the vast majority of breakups do not follow such a convenient path. Unlike in real life, most of the time metaphorical rain is an unwelcome visitor.

In a welcome rainy event the benefit is easy to identify: the trick is to see the benefits in the rain that is unwanted. In the above example at the doctor's office, did you spin it negatively, as an inconvenience upon your lifestyle, or positively, realizing that improving yourself will benefit you in the long run? The trick is to find the benefit in unwelcome rain and travel down that path.

The rains of life will come about on a regular basis, that is for certain: it's just the way life works itself out. Some would say the rains are payback for a past indiscretion on your part, such as the concept of Karma. I suppose that is possible, but whether you deserve the rain or not does not change the process: rains will come, that is a guarantee. The important part is how you deal with life's inevitable watering of your soul.

At the end of the day, it isn't about not having rain: it's about what we do with the rain that has squarely presented itself. It's your choice, but be careful: your decision is going to take you down a path. Make sure this path leads to health, wealth, and longevity of life. All rain has value: you just have to find it.

In a Nutshell

In a literal sense, rain is essential to supporting life as we know it. In most cases, it is very easy for an individual to see the benefits of the watering taking place outside. Although it can be a disappointment if today's activity was supposed to be a round of golf or a sunny picnic, internally we accept that rain is necessary. Most of the time, rain is a gentle force, but occasionally it carries destruction with it.

In our personal lives, we will also experience rain, this time in the form of challenges. Just like in the natural world, they are accepted as necessary but mostly viewed as inconvenient. Occasionally, the storms of life can be quite damaging, and appear to be too much for us to handle. But the natural world always bounces back and so should we. I realize that seeing light at the end of the tunnel can be difficult at times, but that does not mean that it is not there.

Rains are a part of life. It's not so much what happens to us, but how we react that is key. It's okay to be a little frustrated at the inconvenience of a particular rain, but not okay to not want it to rain at all!

Helpful Exercise

If we can accept the fact that rain has value, the obvious goal becomes to identify the benefits that may not be present as we speak, but will grow as a result of our current "rainy" event.

If you are not experiencing some metaphorical rain right now, you might want to put this exercise in your pocket for a later date.

The metaphorical rain I am currently experiencing is:

_____

_____

The benefits that will be realized as a result of this current watering are:

1) _____

2) _____

3) _____

It may be difficult to come up with a possible benefit at first glance, especially if this rainy event is causing some frustration. That frustration can cause you to ignore the benefits that could and should be logical outcomes, so watch out for it.

Think hard, because the future benefits are
inevitably there for the taking.

Some people feel the rain. Others just get wet!

Bob Marley

Chapter Four

ALLOW THE PAST TO INFLUENCE, NOT CONTROL

ALTHOUGH I COMPLETELY agree that our past plays an influential role in the shaping of our future, it in no way architects our future. I have been quite open with the fact that, during my teenage years, I made a few bad choices and found myself on the wrong side of the law. Nothing too dramatic, although they are scenarios I would change given the opportunity. But just because I created a few brushes with the law doesn't mean that I was doomed to a life of criminal activity.

In my case, it was quite the opposite: it didn't take me long to figure out that my path wasn't leading me to a positive outcome. In my case, it propelled me in the opposite direction.

My eyes having been opened to the errors of my ways, I spent my early twenties working with teenagers as a youth leader in conjunction with my new wife, Coleen. I then moved to spending my adult life assisting others in achieving the lives they dream about.

The person you are today is influenced by the person you were in the past. Therefore, the person you will be in the future is influenced by the person you are today.

It should be noted that I am using the word "influenced," not "controlled." My few brushes with the law as a youth did not make me a lifelong criminal, but it influenced me to become quite the opposite. Your past simply influences you; the direction you take is still your choice. You are not a victim of circumstance; it's your choice which path you continue down.

And even after you choose, it doesn't matter how far you go down that path; once you realize it's the wrong one, you can turn around and go back. Nobody is perfect; we have all made choices that, given the opportunity, we would have made differently—in some cases a complete 180.

Your past decisions are not set in granite; it's not like that. Your life is more like clay: it's pliable. Me, you, everyone: we are all works in progress. And yes, we all make bad decisions on occasion. Understand that a less-than-desirable decision is made of clay. Glean whatever positive lessons you can from it, smash it against a tree, and move on with your life. Your decision isn't made of granite: it won't still be intact after its collision with the tree.

Don't allow a poorly-formed clay pot to control the person you are today. Your past only has the right to influence your present.

Everyone has regrets; in fact, I have many. You and I are probably similar in that way. Having regrets is one thing; living in them is quite another. The healthy question to ask yourself is, "What can I learn from this clay-like mistake before I hurl it off that tree?" Then make peace, fire away, and move along with your amazing life.

It would be difficult to maximize your life while carting around huge chunks of granite. They should have been viewed as clay and smashed to smithereens. If this is you, stop right now. Convert that granite to clay and take it out on some poor tree.

As I write this book, cars with the ability to drive themselves are coming onto the scene. Although that will make life interesting in the future, your life path will never be like that. No one can drive your life unless you give them permission to do so. You are squarely in control of your own speed and direction.

Likewise, at a crossroads the direction you choose is entirely up to you. Loved ones will be there to encourage you in a direction, but only you can choose the path. They can travel with you, and that's their choice too, but whatever path you choose is entirely up to you.

Human beings have a tendency to blame others, be it another person or a past self. However, the path you are on was chosen by you. Others may have influenced your decision for sure; however, they did not choose *for* you.

You are also the person in control of whether you allow yourself to be bogged down with mistakes: chunks of granite that should be converted into clay and thrown like with your best fast ball. When something is done, it's done; make restitution and move along. No good can come from dwelling on a mistake.

To some extent, today we deal with the ramifications of the decisions we made in the past. This also means that our tomorrow will be influenced by our decision-making process today. What concerns me is when folks make the mistake of wallowing in regret over something long gone by. If our today is consumed with a past event, and our tomorrow is influenced by our today, that event is being given three lives: in our past, our present, and our future. If it's not on the positive list, we should only allow it the one life: the past.

Forgive and move on; life is too short to grant a negative experience more than one opportunity. Although many circumstances can interrupt your progress, none can do so better than the lack of forgiveness.

When I say "forgiveness" I mean the ability to forgive yourself, to forgive someone else, or to ask for forgiveness. It's time: give forgiveness it's due, and move on to the awesome life that awaits you.

There is an amazing story about a Native American chief that I find inspiring. In an interview, he tells a story of a good dog sitting on one shoulder and a bad dog perched on the other. Both dogs are actively barking instructions into his ears. The interviewer inquires as to which dog usually wins. His response is life changing: "Whichever dog I feed!"

The question you should be asking yourself is this: have you made the popular mistake of dwelling on an issue for too long, giving it extra life? Have you been inadvertently feeding the bad dog?

A chief thief of dreams is time spent dwelling on negative past (or present) circumstances. Life is full of good and bad, ups and downs: that's life. Truthfully, I think you should want it that way. Working through challenges and experiencing those "rainy days" builds character. Without adversity, it's difficult to grow.

It's important to understand that our past does in no way control our future; you are the person that has that control. I would suggest you use it wisely.

In a Nutshell

We are like clay: pliable and easy to shape into a desired result. Our past, at times, can be a hindrance if we don't fully comprehend how it can influence our future. We sometimes think "I have the life I have because of this event in my past." That is not entirely true: although your past influences your future, you and you alone are the architect of what's happening in your life.

Helpful Exercise

Let's take a look at your recent behaviour. Now, please be honest with yourself. I don't have a motive beyond assisting you in achieving the desired life you are searching for. Part of my job is to shine a spotlight on something that may have been hindering your forward progress.

One of these obstacles can be a situation or two that you have allowed to reach a level in your mind that it does not deserve. Is there something that truthfully is no longer a part of your life—an event of your past that, for the sake of your future, you need to let go of? If that's true, let's identify it and take some steps to eliminate it from your life.

Ask yourself:

What have I mistakenly allowed to occupy my mind?

_____

_____

To help identify whether this event is something that is unwanted from your past, ask yourself the following questions:

Am I still involved in this situation?

_____

Is it something positive I want to take with me?

_____

Does this really affect my life? Or have I only allowed it to?

_____

What can I do to prevent it from affecting my future?

_____

_____

Solution:

_____ is not important to me from this day forward.

Who controls the past controls the future: who controls the present controls the past.

George Orwell

Chapter Five

SLOW DOWN

AT FIRST GLANCE, it may appear that the topic for this chapter conflicts with the concept of this book, *It's Time: Your Awesome Life Awaits*. In fact, quite the opposite is true: they support and depend upon each other.

If we were constantly moving forward in order to achieve our dreams, we would, in fact, likely fail. In order to achieve a desired goal, we must slow down on a regular basis and mentally exhale.

When someone opens up and shares their worthwhile goal, my heart leaps with excitement for them. I want to know more: what's their timeline? Interestingly, it is this question that is often the most difficult to answer, and at that point I realize that this particular dream has been occupying mental space for some time. And it likely will remain that way until they outline a plan for themselves, including both the steps they wish to take and the times of rest in between.

When you embark on a road trip, you don't drive for 3 days straight. First off, it would be dangerous if you tried. And secondly, you wouldn't enjoy yourself. Resting is part of a road trip; in fact, it's taking advantage of those rest stops that makes the trip enjoyable. You stop for gas, food, scenic lookouts, and overnight lodging. It's all part of the overall process.

In the success world, it's exactly like that: if you try to drive yourself straight to your goal, you will never make it. So to reach the amazing goals you have set for yourself, you have to take the same steps as a road trip: get to know your destination, load up the car, and only get on the road. And be patient: you can't arrive today. So just like you would pre-plan some stops on your road trip, do the same with mental breaks toward your goal. How quickly you arrive isn't as important as the fact that you ultimately arrive.

As an example, as of the writing of this book, my company is on an upward trajectory. Therefore, the logical goal is to double up on the company. I'm very careful to allow time for that process. I suppose I could focus on achieving that in a one-year period—truth be told, I could probably do that. But I wouldn't be adhering to any of the success principles I teach. It would be detrimental to me and likely my company. In order to fast-track my goal I would probably be required to sacrifice other aspects of my life, which would, in the long run, put me in a worse position.

So rather than compressing my goal into a twelve-month period, why not spread it out over three years and purposefully enjoy the ride? Wouldn't it be smarter to plan for a lot of down time, and put a few scenic lookouts into the schedule? I'm still going to arrive. It may take a little longer, but that is fine by me. Better to enjoy the ride.

Ask yourself an honest question. Which would be better: A) to take three relaxing days and arrive calm, refreshed, and safe, or B) to hop yourself up on coffee and Red Bull so that you can drive for two straight days, only to be forced to sleep for a full day to recuperate? Obviously, option "A" is the way to go.

Just like the road trip, we need to plan time for relaxation and mental exhales. Fortunately for me, I have a year-round cottage about 90 minutes from my house in the city. Regardless of how much is on the go, I spend several days there mentally exhaling. This is where all my writing takes place. There is something about nature that inspires my creative energy.

My mental exhales are built into my lifestyle. When I return to the office on Monday morning, my batteries are recharged. I should point out that this is my schedule regardless of the goals that draw on my time. Life always comes first.

You will have to decide for yourself how to build in mental exhales. We have many clients that simply turn their phones off several nights a week. Others play golf, go fishing, or spend an afternoon gardening; it's really up to what you want to do to recharge your batteries.

In life, there is a time to go and a time to hold back. Consider for a moment a horse race. Right out the gate it's time to go: the jockey pushes the horse down the first quarter mile. Come the second and third quarters, however, they hold the horse back. Finally, when they come around the clubhouse turn, it's time to go again, and they push the horse for all it has.

The reason the jockey holds the horse back during the 2nd and 3rd quarters is because they are well aware that the horse is incapable of sprinting the entire mile.

There is a great lesson for us here: you are incapable of sprinting directly to your goal. Even if you could, you would arrive exhausted. Instead, you should allocate a little more time for the process and arrive refreshed, possessing many awesome memories of the excursion. The point isn't to set realistic goals in an unrealistic timeframe. This creates stress, high blood pressure, and a host of other physical repercussions.

When we try to sprint directly to our goal, we tend to take on a "go it alone" attitude. This blocks others out as we attempt to sprint past them. On the other hand, when we allocate more time to the process and accept the fact that rest and enjoyment are built in along the way, we automatically include others in our quest. Life's better together.

We are very conscious of this particular concept at Rob Vivian Coaching. When we assist our valued clients in the setting of their annual goals, we first check to make sure said goal has included the necessary time for ample rest. Secondly, we inquire as to whether or not they have consulted their loved ones regarding their upcoming venture; in most cases, this important step has been overlooked.

As part of my job, I point out that their odds of success are higher if they build in some extra time for rest and fun along the way. In most cases, other people are part of that fun. So why not consult those people who would be present?

If you really think about it, the goals we set are often to benefit others around us. We shouldn't be in a hurry to get there: it's better on every level if we take our time, rest on a regular basis, and enjoy the ride. Life is not about the destination, it's about the journey.

It's funny: when I quote that in a seminar, the entire audience whole-heartedly agrees: it's about the journey, not the destination. And yet when we set our goals, we attempt to achieve the exact opposite. Unless we also set our intent to enjoy the journey, we will inevitably end up with the same result we have earlier achieved: failure!

In a Nutshell

Sometimes, through an over-eager mindset, we can make the all-too-common mistake of driving ourselves single-mindedly to our worthwhile goals. On the outside, this may appear like a good idea: to arrive as quickly as possible. But in fact, this is not beneficial. After all, life is about the journey, not the destination. Take some extra time to allow for side experiences. It's often those unexpected experiences that add value to our journey.

Don't always be in a hurry to get somewhere. We all know our lives will end at some point: let's not be in a hurry to get there. Slow down a bit, take your time, and add in new and exciting scenarios.

Helpful Exercise

It's easy to *say* slow down a bit, take a breath, and take in some scenery along the way. The harder question for you to ask yourself is: what is that scenery? What could happen at those extra stops? For me, these are easy: fishing, hockey, golf, and being at the lake.

My question to you, then, is what are *your* mental exhales? Remember that those rest spots should be happening on a regular basis, not once and a while.

The exercise, then, is to list three things that you really enjoy and honestly don't spend near enough time doing!

Item #1 _____

Item #2 _____

Item #3 _____

Don't sell yourself on the made-up story that your busy schedule
simply doesn't allow you to have the time. That's not true:
we always find time for the things we enjoy.

Don't be in a hurry to achieve your dreams. Take a day to play with your kids and relax—your dreams will still be there tomorrow.

Lindsey Rietzsch

Chapter Six

DO WHAT YOU KNOW IS RIGHT

MOST PEOPLE WHO are inspired to accomplish a worthwhile goal set a plan in motion and off they go. Of course, I encourage the idea of creating a plan prior to embarking on your quest. But even I will admit that most people do not give enough thought to the moral principles that will either empower you or, in some cases, hinder you along your way.

This chapter will serve to enlighten you. This principle of doing what you know is right will propel you toward your ideal outcome. On the other hand, if you accidentally make a poor decision that causes you to stray from your moral compass (regardless of the rationalization used) it will act as a cement block and drag you down.

There is no doubt that you will be presented with many forks in the road, and sometimes one of those directions leads to a lack of integrity. Often, you will be acutely aware that it is incorrect. You may rationalize your choice by saying "No one will know," or "It's not that wrong, really; I'm not hurting anyone."

Sometimes, your easy-to-persuade mind will convince you that the high road, laced with integrity, is definitely the longer route. You may tell yourself, "This route does lead in the direction of my goal. However, it appears to meander a bit; maybe that shortcut on the left is a bit more direct. After all, nobody is going to get hurt!"

Here's the thing with turning in the direction that compromises your integrity: when you make a decision that demonstrates a lack of integrity (however minor it may appear), your success suffers. This occurs whether you get caught or not. Certainly, if you are exposed, you may be in trouble or simply embarrassed. However, let me be clear: your punishment in the success world remains the same. If you make a decision that shows a lack of integrity, the success world will punish you proportionately. It's as simple as that.

On the other hand, when you make a decision to do what you know is right, those obstacles that once appeared to hinder your path will, in fact, prove a reward for maintaining your personal integrity. Am I saying that all morally correct decisions have a benefit attached? Correct! The benefit or punishment may not be immediate, but don't fool yourself. In the success world, your intentions are noted.

As we travel through this wonderful life, we will find ourselves at this particular crossroads regularly. When you take the less moral path, it doesn't make you a bad person: it makes you a good person making a bad decision. All too often, this will be due to an impatient nature in your quest to achieve your life's ambitions.

Just because it's time to get started on the awesome life that awaits you doesn't mean you should make a quick, impatient turn in an attempt to get to your goal today. I encourage you to get started, certainly, because you have probably been thinking about accomplishing your goal for quite some time. And in most cases, getting started will squarely place you at a fork in the road. A decision will have to be made without delay, but that does not mean you should choose the fastest route—not if it betrays your principles.

Although the decision that supports your personal integrity does not always appear to be the long and winding road, in most cases it will. Since you should be enjoying the ride anyway, that shouldn't be perceived as a problem. The truth is, when you make a decision that goes against your morals, you will find no enjoyment there. You may pretend to be surprised when you are later exposed; however, in your heart you were aware the entire time.

If we continually choose the immoral path, we will eventually develop characteristics that obstruct us from becoming successful. It's not an immediate transformation; however, over time we will become a person who possesses an anxious spirit, one who is very familiar with stress and other negative attributes. We will eventually become a cynical person, rendering our life's aspirations into a virtual impossibility. Like any true cynic, you would make up untrue stories to explain away others' successes and justify your own lack.

Integrity is what you do when no one is looking. It is how you conduct yourself in secret. You can, and probably will, fool everyone around you, but the success world will not be fooled. I wonder, sometimes, how many good, caring folks make this simple mistake. The principle is absolute: you make a decision that lacks integrity, and the success world bites you. You make a decision full of integrity, and the success world honours that in some form or another.

It is also true that the correct decision may not always be a popular one; others may question the choice you have made. When this happens—and it will—you must understand that the vast majority of those who dwell on Earth are not experiencing anything that even resembles success. Without a doubt, this is the moral principle at work. Today, we live in a society where everyone believes that what they think is correct and what everyone else thinks is somehow flawed. Here's a news flash: you are not the most important person on the planet!

Decisions that possess honesty and integrity are the direction to take in life. I realize that most people feel very differently. However, the very reason you are reading this book is your desire to separate yourself from the pack.

Take your time and make the decision to take the more enjoyable, scenic route that adheres to your moral principles. You'll know it, because it will be the route that you heart tells you is correct, even though no one would be aware you had chosen that route over the other. The success world would know.

If you purposefully choose to take the correct path—the path filled with adventure—you eventually become magnetic to others. When I say "magnetic," I mean exactly that: you will attract others to you, based on the principle of the law of attraction. As a calm person, you will be viewed as supportive and knowledgeable, the kind of person those in need turn to.

In all likelihood, I'm describing the person you desire to become. If that's true, don't take the tempting turn: the one that appears to be a faster, less honest route to your goal. It's a trap most have fallen victim to. Instead, take a breath and choose the route you know is right.

This particular topic is mostly a matter of mindset. Learn to make the decision that leans toward integrity. Stop analyzing your odds of getting caught and start making better choices: choices that truly line up with your personal character.

If you are in the sales industry, it's a well-known fact that people do business with those they like. In fact, whether you sell vacuum cleaners, insurance, farm equipment, or real estate, I'm willing to bet that you are already familiar with this idea. Until now, you have probably thought the concept was exclusive to your particular industry. News flash: it's a characteristic of human behaviour. In fact, people will willingly and eagerly pay more for your product if they like you on top of seeing the value in whatever you're selling.

When you are a person who does the right thing, both in your manner of thinking and how you conduct yourself, others will sense that on an instinctual level—it's almost a sixth sense.

You cannot fake this attribute: you either live by this rule or you do not. I'm sure we've all had the scenario where we were interacting with a salesperson who wanted us to purchase their product, but something deep inside us was screaming not to buy from this person. We do want the product, but there is something about this person that sets off every alarm we have. They may be smiling, listening to our concerns, and asking the right questions, yet there is something not right about this person!

I'm suggesting that your subconscious is picking up on a simple fact: the sales person smiling at you from the other side of the table is not interested in you or your needs at all. More often than not, they have been travelling down the immoral path. Their focus is not the customer, it's the sales. Their friendly manner and the shininess of their shoes may fool you on the outside, but your inner discerning sense will not be fooled. Follow your gut, thank them for their time, and find someone that cares about you.

I can't really say what percentage of salespeople make decisions that are correct for the client and what percentage are looking out for number one. It's safe to say that the vast majority, albeit good people, are more concerned about their quantity of sales than their number of happy customers. They may be smooth enough to fool you on the outside, but if their presentation is insincere, you'll possess a nagging feeling that indicates something isn't quite right.

It goes without saying that this type of salesperson will struggle in achieving their desired goals. In my travels I see this a lot. Interestingly, they think that they need to work on their presentation—that the presentation must be the part that is not strong enough. All the while, what is actually missing is their integrity and a genuine client-first mindset.

On the other side of the coin, salespeople that travel the path of integrity and put their clients' interests ahead of their own achieve an amazing connection with those clients. On the outside, everything is exactly the same: their shoes are shiny, there's lots of smiling and listening. But along with the quality presentation, your inner voice will be urging you to pick this person. Even if they are a bit more expensive, you know it's well worth it.

People do business with those they like. Everyone responds well to a professional presentation that is coupled with an inner attraction to your honest personality. And it all happens at the subconscious level. The client really isn't aware that their personal assessing system is picking up on the integrity (or lack thereof) from you as a presenter. What they may verbalize is "I feel comfortable with you," or "I feel like you care."

It's worth mentioning again that you cannot fake this part of the interaction: you either care about those you are interacting with, or you are solely focused on your own benefit.

I own a real estate coaching company, so most of my examples come from the literally thousands of real estate sales people I interact with annually. It's amazing how often I get asked to assist with presentation delivery, and yet to date not one Realtor has asked me for some integrity coaching.

People do business with people they like. If you are squarely focused on personal sales, having them like you on a subconscious level would be virtually impossible.

Let's take a look at a non-business example. How does this topic connect to parenting, for instance? Choosing the path of integrity probably isn't always the popular choice. As parents, we are tempted to be too flexible. After all, who doesn't want to be the cool parent? But keep in mind, it's your job to raise good children into good adults.

Taking your family down a path of integrity will run squarely in the face of popular thinking. For instance, I had a 6-year-old tell me the other day that he was hoping to get a cell phone for Christmas, because all his friends already had one. That's a lot of cool parents! I noticed a group of 15 or so young people, no more than 12 years old, at the mall being openly disrespectful to those around them—more cool parents!

Making the right choices and guiding a family down the path of integrity will undoubtedly induce some friction. For a time, your children may feel like they are the only ones not allowed to participate in some activities. However, let me be clear: it's your job as a parent to do the right thing. Your children may not like it now, but believe me when I tell you, your integrity will resonate with them over time. I doubt they will express that thought to you in the beginning; however, you can be sure it is making the point where it matters.

Over time, they will instinctively know the right path because you have taken a stance and pointed them toward it. They will probably never say, "okay, you were correct; my mistake," when their teenage friends spend an unsupervised weekend alone and they're stuck watching a movie with the family. They won't be happy, but deep down they know you chose the right path.

Down the road they will be making their own choices. There is no habit better than a habit of good choices. Don't try to be the cool parent: be the correct parent!

When I say it's time because your awesome life awaits, I mean that on many levels. In this case, it's time to make the right decisions for you, your family, and your success.

In a Nutshell

When we encounter that all-too-familiar moral choice, we have an important decision to make. Do we lean toward what we know in our hearts to be correct, or do we once again try to explain away why it's okay to sacrifice our integrity? You can tell yourself that no one is going to get hurt and that your indiscretion will remain secret. But your success will be affected just the same, and your decisions will become either a blessing or a stumbling block.

If your decision is immoral, regardless of the level of your indiscretion, you will be punished on a level proportionate to your incorrect choice. Obviously, your reward for making a moral decision will be proportionate to the integrity you applied. I'm sure you are a good person at your core, so one way to identify a wrong decision is if you find yourself rationalizing your position. Most good choices don't require rationalizing.

In your quest to get on with the awesome life that awaits you, a common setback is the constant struggle of fighting through the repercussions of selfish decisions. You can never achieve the ultimate, awesome life that is meant for you that way. Do what you know is right and put yourself on the path to success.

Helpful Exercise

So that we're clear, I in no way doubt your positive qualities. You are an impressive individual. Honestly, I probably believe in you more than you believe in yourself. However, in our haste toward accomplishment we often find ourselves rationalizing why it's okay to make a decision that we know in our heart is incorrect. Just because we are not hurting someone does not make it okay.

Although I may be travelling down several incorrect paths, my most predominant error is:

_____

_____

The wrong decision I made was:

_____

I have been justifying it as:

_____

What I need to do instead is:

_____

Now that we have acknowledged the immoral decision, let's travel back to the fork in the road and take the correct route. I realize you may be on the wrong path in multiple areas of your life, but it's best to fix them one at a time.

It doesn't matter how far you have travelled down a path; once you realize it's the incorrect one, immediately go back.

Honesty and integrity are absolutely essential for success in life—all areas of life. The really good news is that anyone can develop both honesty and integrity.

Zig Ziglar

Chapter Seven

THE JOY IS IN THE NOW

AS I WROTE this chapter, I realized that this concept finds its way into all my books, and will most likely be woven into the pages of my future writings. In fact, I am presently scheduled to conduct several hundred seminars annually. This idea, that "the joy is in the now," continually comes up. I guess no matter whether I'm writing or speaking, it is indisputable in my mind that although our future is an amazing place, we do not live there yet. Right now the "amazing" that exists in our life exists in the awesome now.

That awesome future is exactly that: an awesome *future*. Today, we are limited to dreaming about it. I hope that all your joy isn't relegated to a future date. I trust that you, like me, share that joy around, applying a good portion to the future while experiencing ample portions of it in the here and now.

As an example, let's say your life vision is to use your skills in the medical field: perhaps as a doctor, as a nurse, or maybe in the field of research. I can imagine that those who pursue this particular field have a noble plan to assist others. It's a magical thing, really, to be in a position to play a part in another human being's wellness. To be that surgeon who walks confidently into a waiting room and informs the overwhelmed family that everything is going to be okay, and they can see their loved one shortly.

A medical student probably dreams about that opportunity to make a significant difference. But today is day one of med school, and that opportunity resides in the distant future. For today, we need to take the necessary steps to gain the knowledge and experience required to be called upon on this family's desperate day. As awesome as that will be, that situation is years down the road. Therefore, we have to find a way to share the magnitude of that experience with not only our future, but our present. It would be a mistake to save all our exhilaration for a future date and miss the amazing of the now.

The joy of being in the now is a conscious thought. The onus is on us to realize that although achieving our amazing future holds a place in our hearts, life takes place today.

I am very fortunate that I, personally, have the blessed opportunity to play a small part in assisting business people with their goals and dreams. I am acutely aware that most of my clients will automatically apply all their satisfaction to a future date. On one hand, it does improve their focus; on the other hand, it will inevitably rob them of the joy in the now. It's a balancing act, really.

On some levels, speakers and writers like me are partly to blame for this unfortunate mistake. I commonly sit in on other speakers' presentations. Sometimes, I hear a message that I realize could be inadvertently damaging to the listener. I am 100% confident that the presenter in no way intended to create a stumbling block for the participant. But messages like "never give up on your dreams," "work hard now for a payoff in the future," or "focus on your amazing future," although great talks—I myself use them on occasion—can be taken to extreme if not tempered.

When I hear one of these inspiring and motivational topics about one's awesome future, I am always waiting for the presenter to wrap up with, "Always remember that that is the future. You live in the now, the now should be just as exciting as your perfect future."

Sometimes, when the mention of the present goes unsaid, and the presenter wraps up to a well-deserved applause, I take out my phone and make a note to ensure I don't forget to reinforce that the joy is in the now in my next, similar, talk. The last thing I want is to influence people to become so excited about their perfect future that they don't leave any excitement for their present.

As you read this, you could fall into several different categories: 1) All fired up about your awesome future, with no regard for the present. Sadly, there is no joy in this scenario. Hold on to those future thoughts and add in the amazing present.

2) Excited about your present with little consideration for your future path. This situation will have joy now, but it would be tenfold if you were clear with yourself about your amazing future.

3) Not excited about your now with no vision for the future. This one has to change, and you are the one to change it. I am not saying that your current situation is your fault. Whether you got here from situations inside or outside of your control doesn't matter. What is your call is whether you are staying here. You may not have put yourself in your circumstances, but you are the one who decides whether or not to stay.

No matter your category, there are only two steps you have to follow. First, create a dream. Visualize where you will be assuming everything will go your way. Take that first step toward your amazing future. Second, count your blessings today and live with them in your mind. Get excited about your amazing future, all the while revelling in the joy of the now.

A common example of this process is regarding a person's physical condition and weight. Let's pretend you are male and your scale is currently communicating to you that you are carrying around 210lbs. You step on and off several times just to make sure the scale is not malfunctioning. It isn't. But 180lbs was the message you were hoping to get. So now you have your goal. The same principle applies here: make a plan, implement some changes, and count your current blessings as you embark on a path to your desired 180lbs. The joy is in the now!

You can't reserve all your excitement for that future day when the scale reads 180. This journey will have lots of small accomplishments along the way, especially the first time you crack the 200lbs marker. Logically, your mind can visualize the satisfaction of reaching the goal *and* some of the smaller increments of success along the way.

It is also necessary to find some joy in your current reality of 210 pounds. Finding an angle you like in the mirror, even sporting those extra pounds, is a good place to start. However, let's say that's a little difficult, since 180 is your ideal. This is when we should be considering other parts of your body beyond the "all-important" physical appearance. Let's say your heart is strong and, aside from the extra weight, you are in very good health. If you had a choice of extra weight or a bad heart, I'm sure you would choose the extra weight on all the days that end with "y." So let's start there: you are in great health. That's awesome. The joy is in the now.

I would even go so far to say that your amazing future holds very little value if you ignore your amazing now. It is always a good time to take a minute to take stock of the current circumstances that really make up who you are.

This topic, enjoying where you are now, comes up a lot in popular culture and Hollywood movies. Tell me if you've seen this one before: a high level executive with little time for anything but work finds herself in a small town for Christmas, where she realizes that there is more to life than the promotion that is constantly being dangled in front of her at the office. As you know, the movie always ends with the lead character rediscovering the benefits of living in the now, realizing there is more to life than the possibility of future benefit.

I should say two things in my defence: number one, I mean no disrespect to high-achiever executive types. In fact, I am one. I'm just saying that losing touch with the awesome present is a mistake. Secondly, I'm clearly watching way too many holiday movies with my wife!

In a Nutshell

The true joy of life is the exhilaration of living in the now: of being completely content in the present moment. Therefore, when asked by others, "Hey, how's it going?" your automatic response of, "Great!" will be an honest answer (as it should). I am, of course, a big—no, let me upgrade that to huge—believer in setting astronomical goals for you and your family. But I'm not a supporter of living solely in your awesome future at the expense of all the amazing present that takes place around you on a daily basis. In fact, in my humble opinion, I believe that enjoying the now, and only periodically visiting your desired future, is the correct approach.

So fully immerse yourself in the joy of the now, while stopping to visit your perfect future on a regular basis. Mentally draw power from an amazing destination, then return to your current life.

You'll find that at times it is so amazing it becomes difficult to hide your exuberance. The joy of life is living in an amazing present that is fuelled by an exhilarating future.

Helpful Exercise

You know I am a believer in goal setting: I don't think I need to sell you on that fact. However, should we really ignore all the amazing aspects of life that we currently possess? It's not a good idea to be so future-oriented that you lose out on the incredible now!

Let's take a few minutes and itemize some of those awesome components that make up our incredible present. Focus on those items that occasionally get pushed to the side or perhaps ignored with a little too much forward thinking.

List three things that truly make your current life amazing:

Amazing Item #1 _____

Amazing Item #2 _____

Amazing Item #3 _____

If you carry joy in your heart, you can heal any moment.

Carlos Santana

Chapter Eight

REFLECT A LOT

THE VAST MAJORITY of our past falls squarely into the category of situations that we cherish: circumstances that, when thought upon, bring a smile to our face. These fond memories play a significant part in shaping the person we have become. They should be reflected upon regularly; so much so that a day should not pass without some quiet contemplation.

Particularly in the success world, there is a big push to get everywhere in a big hurry. Now, I should say that I am a believer in striving to improve ourselves every day we breathe. Life is so incredibly valuable that not even one day should be wasted. We should purposefully keep our forward momentum. However, that momentum should not be at the expense of meaningful past experiences.

As an example, if you have had the good fortune of bringing children into this world, that is a forever life-changing day. For the ladies, I'm quite sure you were just thankful when the process was finally complete. You had put all the uncomfortable days and the travails of childbirth behind you and arrived at a moment that no words can properly describe: of holding your newborn to your chest. If you find yourself on the male side of the equation, it's that moment of pure pride when you are informed whether it's a girl or a boy. What an amazing day!

You wouldn't want this memory to fade: the correct move is to store this moment in a safe, accessible location of your brain. That way, it can be easily located in times of turmoil, when reflection on a positive event in your life is required. Maybe it's nothing more than a difficult day at the office, or maybe it's a more serious, life-altering change. Either way, pulling out positive memories from your vast reservoir of uplifting experiences can be immensely helpful. But this benefit can only be experienced by those who have purposefully taken the time to reflect regularly on the multiple experiences they have accumulated over time, which allows the memories to be easily accessed on a difficult day.

We can and should draw upon these positive events for encouragement when we are on the right track or require a push to propel ourselves over the finish line. Or perhaps we need it because we took a wrong turn and require some uplifting energy from a positive experience in order to get ourselves back to the fork in the road and take a new path.

There are, of course, certain memories where the correct move is to put them squarely in the rear view mirror, never to be revisited. These items could have been your mistake, or perhaps they happened through no fault of your own; either way, the past is the past. If a particular item falls into the category of your doing, make mental restitution (remember to practise forgiveness) and move along. I often say to those people holding on to a mistake, "You only have to apologize once. Then move along." To sincerely apologize and then purposefully live in that mistake is a dangerous situation. What's done is done: make amends and move forward, physically and, most importantly, mentally.

Many amazing things have happened in our lives. I mentioned the birth of your children as an example, but maybe you look fondly upon your wedding day. Or perhaps you found yourself involved in a vitally-important social program where others were helped by your efforts at what they would consider a desperate time in their lives. As you reflect on your contribution, it is difficult not to feel a strong sense of accomplishment. These important parts of our lives are where we draw strength and purpose. In my humble opinion, it would be a shame to travel down a path fully focused on the future and ignore all the good from the past.

When a worthwhile goal is accomplished, there is no doubt that we have created a memory that can be reflected on for a sense of motivation and accomplishment. It is a resource to draw courage from in our future endeavours, for sure. Along the way, smaller accomplishments will stack together to make up the overall accomplishment. Those smaller pieces of the puzzle possess great value.

Perhaps your goal is to regain the trust of a child whose relationship with you has landed on challenging ground. Once the relationship has been fully repaired, obviously life will operate on a much improved level; however, it should be pointed out that along the way smaller gains will be achieved. Those special moments should not be passed by quickly. Time should be spent there in quiet contemplation to consider your small success. The relationship is not yet where it needs to be, but maybe a civil conversation took place. In all likelihood, others will follow.

Once the relationship is fully restored, life will operate on a higher personal level; however, without acknowledging those previous, smaller successes you might not hold up your side in the restoration of a relationship. If your viewpoint is to celebrate once the goal has been completed, ignoring the fuel supplied along the way, you will most likely run out of gas before you reach your destination.

When planning a road trip, you would never attempt to complete the excursion without fuelling up. If 2,000 kilometres have to be covered and your tank only lasts for 500, fuelling up is second nature. We should take that thinking into our goal setting. Fuel up often. Stop for a bit when a small accomplishment has been completed: don't just drive by the gas station.

To get in a habit of participating in quiet time, give yourself a timeout. We live in a world filled with ever-increasing distractions, most of which are at our fingertips. We can no longer sit still and reflect; there always seems to be something interesting on our phones, something like a group chat that our brains tell us is important to participate in.

A couple of years ago, I realized half way home from the cottage that I had forgotten my phone at the lake. I thought, "Should I go back? I'm only 45 minutes from the lake. It is Monday, but there's a long weekend coming up, so I will be returning Thursday. Really, it's only 3 days." I decided to live without my phone for 3 days, and guess what? It was awesome.

I should say that since my social media presence is limited—I'm an analog person in a digital world—it would have been easier for me than another who is in the habit of keeping up a daily social media presence. However, even though I'm a person that has limited interest in social media, I do read the news, check stocks, text, and return email. I noticed that when I was sitting idle, I often reached for my phone only to realize once again that it was enjoying some quiet time at the lake.

My point is, even though I spend minimal time on social media I still allow it to infringe on, and effectively steal, my valuable quiet time. Since those 3 days I have made a few subtle changes in my life, one of which is to make sure I sit quietly for a few minutes every day and reflect on all the awesome in my life. I didn't realize how much that little mechanical device had replaced the value of reflection. Scrolling with your thumb is not quiet reflection.

Seeing as I am one of the very few living outside the social media infatuation, I imagine your device is probably causing the same problem.

Your past is you and that's the way it is. No doubt we all would love to visit our past selves and make some changes. Since that cannot be done, all our amazing past decisions and accomplishments are there to stay right beside all the gaffes we made. These are the elements that make up the person your friends and relatives love, so accept all of it.

I encounter people whose goal is to make themselves into a whole new person. But the idea is to make a *better* you, not a new you. Therefore, it concerns me when I encounter a person who cannot itemize amazing scenarios from their past. Somehow, someway, they have sold themselves on the idea that their past has no value: that all their value lies in their perfect future. But this is not the case, and should not be thought of in that way.

Instead, I get them to tell me about the things that they love about themselves. Next, we reflect on the amazing accomplishments from their past. Some people have tried their best to sell me on the fact that, for them, these categories are barren. Fortunately for them I am persistent, and within a few minutes I have them expanding on some awesome contributions they have made to this planet.

You should be too: give yourself credit where credit is due; everyone should list at least three things for each question.

Once we itemize a few categories we can begin to add to them, building a better you rather than a new, non-existent person.

I can tell you with all confidence that you are an amazing person. You have so much to offer, and your future will be an amazing one for sure. However, don't undersell your past accomplishments, because they are significant.

Although it is true that always looking forward can be dangerous, it is still where the majority of your attention should be focused. If we revisit the road trip metaphor, the majority of your time should be spent looking out the windshield. It allows you to pay attention to what is coming your way so that you can occasionally detour and bring an interesting experience into your path. That said, it would still be wise to periodically glance in the rear view mirror.

Our lives are exactly like that: mostly forward thinking, but at least once a day we should allocate some time for looking back. Separate yourself from your phone, sit quietly, and reflect. Think about all those amazing scenarios that bring a smile to your face. It's therapy. It won't last, but then, neither does bathing; that's why we do it regularly!

I often reflect on watching the sports my children participated in while they were young. Some people complain about getting up at 6am on a Saturday morning to take a child to hockey, but I suggest that they enjoy it while they can: they're going to miss it when their children grow up. Even though my son Josh is now in his thirties, I still enjoy going to his games periodically. I have equally fond memories of watching my daughter Corissa gracefully land a difficult figure-skating move, and of the pair of them competing in gymnastics.

The point is that these are amazing memories. You have similar ones, so it would be wise to allocate a bit of your day to them. I know this is yet another thing to add to what seems like an ever-increasing demand on your daily schedule. But the onus is on you to make the time: don't think that this worthwhile reflection will happen on its own.

Maybe that's what people mean when they express to me that they feel void of any purpose; maybe, in their quest to achieve something significant, they forgot to use those memorable moments as the fuel they need to complete their journey.

In a Nutshell

The point of this book is to cement in your mind that it's time: your awesome life awaits. These goals have been in your mind for quite awhile, and the time for thinking is over: the time for moving forward is now. However, taking some time every day to reflect on past moments will create positive anchors in your life. Regularly playing these amazing memories in your mind will create immense resilience.

Making a decision to put all past events, both positive and negative, in your metaphorical rear view mirror will leave you shallow, with no sense of purpose. It's these moments that make up who you are: that person whom so many love and look to in times of guidance.

You should spend time daily to reflect on those precious moments from your past. It's up to you to make the necessary time; it definitely will not happen on its own.

Helpful Exercise

It is necessary to take time daily to reflect on precious moments that are stored in our hearts. We would be wise to itemize them and allocate a small chunk of time daily to ponder them.

First, list three things you love about yourself:

Awesome item #1 _____

Awesome item #2 _____

Awesome item #3 _____

Next, list three situations or scenarios that bring great joy when brought to mind:

Joyful Item #1 _____

Joyful Item #2 _____

Joyful Item #3 _____

The final step is to schedule time each day to reflect on these amazing scenarios and strengthen your inner resolve. Although any time would work, I can attest that 5 or 10 minutes in the morning is the easiest to follow.

*"Contentment in your quiet time won't come from
your future but your past."*

You can't hurry creativity, so take time to ponder your ideas.
Sit back and take time to think things over.
That's usually how the best ideas bloom.

Harvey MacKay

Chapter Nine

EMBRACE GENEROSITY

GENEROSITY IS A MANDATORY component in successful goals. A couple of my previous books touch on this fact. My book *Expecting Awesome Daily* explains the state of mind necessary to live and expect something awesome to visit you on a daily basis. Of course, generosity is required to elevate yourself to that state.

Another of my books, *Success Explosion,* covers the attributes that are required to experience a bone fide success explosion in all aspects of your life. And, you guessed it, generosity is a required element there, too.

It's a characteristic that is mandatory for personal growth: it's not the sort of thing you can fake or pretend to be a participant in. You are either a generous person or you are not.

The opposite of generosity is dwelling in a state where you consider yourself to be more important than those around you. It is true that most of the population does, in fact, live in this state, which also explains why so few people experience success in their lifetime.

The lessons in this book are meant to ensure that you are one of those who do move, once and for all, to the higher plane of successful living. Each of us is different, which is why the amazing life that we imagine takes many shapes and sizes. For me, it's always been the dream of having a nice cottage to spend weekends fishing, swimming, or writing—as I am doing at this exact moment!

Throughout my many years of business, my family has grown. My kids are now experienced businesspeople with their own sets of ambitions. I have had numerous "it's time" moments of my own along the way. Although I would not consider myself done, there are probably more "it's time" moments in my past than there are still on my path.

I have been very clear from my late teens that a lake house must be in my future. I have carried that thought with me from the beginning. Many "it's time" moments presented themselves and were successfully conquered to get to my present situation.

It's up to you to figure out what your future will look like: you must have a clear picture of it. Without a clear understanding of what you really want, you won't be able to have an "it's time" experience. It's time for what?

Perhaps you would like to be in a position to pay for your children's post-secondary education, and they are moving toward that date a little faster than you would like. It's time. Maybe, like me, you live in a northern climate that can, at times, be extremely cold. A home or condo in a warmer location would be amazing. It's time. I can't really say what is important to you, I can only say that your life is moving at a rapid pace and you have no time to waste. It's time.

Generosity is a mandatory step to take toward success, although I know that at first glance it can appear backward: that to get more we have to first give things away. Reason suggests that the more I keep, the more I have. But I don't make up the rules of how success works, I just teach them. And the truth is most of the rules of success seem to defy logic.

We can work under only our own power, grinding our way to what we perceive as success. Or we can enlist life's success principles. When we work with only our own strength, we will still likely achieve a level of success; however, we must enlist the appropriate success principles if we desire our success to be on a grand scale.

Think of it this way: if you found yourself rowing a boat across a lake, you would be making progress for sure. However, if you were to raise the sail and catch some wind, that would be much more helpful.

When you take advantage of your "it's time" moments and augment them with the success principles, your journey will be a lot smoother. You may have the strength to row across the entire lake on your own, but I think you'll agree that catching some wind in your sail is very helpful.

The principle of contribution does require some understanding on the participant's part. Your motive determines its effectiveness: you can't give of one of your resources (be it money, time, or skills) just to activate the principle; unfortunately, it doesn't work that way. You must give with a pure heart. If you are giving in order to get, nothing will find its way to you. On the other hand, if you give with a pure heart—one that aligns with a generous spirit—then and only then will this success principle activate.

With that in mind, we should always be on the lookout for opportunities to give from our abundance, and to do so from the goodness of our hearts. When we align with this particular principle, commonly called "The Law of Reciprocity," abundance flows back to us in a much greater quantity than what we gave.

The important part here is to be purely generous. Obviously, if your motive is to give in order to get, you won't be a generous person; you would simply be a person masquerading as a generous person. And trust me, that is nowhere near the same thing.

A non-generous person collects everything for themselves. To me, those that live their lives in a hoarding mindset like this seem to be the most miserable people, even though they have hoarded vast reservoirs of wealth and possessions.

I personally know a few people who fall into this category. They cannot enjoy their wealthy position, nor feel satisfied that what they have stored away is adequate: they always seem to worry about spending when they have enough to last well past what they need. I guess the years of hoarding have created a mindset of "more is never enough."

On the other side of the coin, those that are generous with their resources seem to be the most content. The more generous they are, the less they seem to worry about their future.

You have the choice of which group to reside in. I would highly recommend you choose the group that lives carefree, those who assist those around them as they pass through their days. Your success is designed to free you, not bury you in a collection of wealth.

We all want and should want to move forward in life toward the goals we deem important. I know it sounds odd to step backward and give your resources away, but it is in order to open up forward momentum. Ask any successful person and they will tell you success is not a straight line: that there were many steps they took that temporarily placed the goal further away. But often it was those steps that allowed them to make up ground on a later day.

Successful people understand the Law of Reciprocity, and that they must give back a bit, even when that temporarily delays their ultimate goal. The reason they are willing to accept this temporary setback is because they are doing what they know is right, another success principle. Successful people will make the correct call and give from their reservoir of resources. In comparison, people who do not understand the benefit of generosity lock down their assets and continue rowing across the lake on their windless day.

The principle of generosity is an attribute you choose whether or not to participate in. I'm not saying that if you make the incorrect decision to keep your assets to yourself that you will not experience success at some level; of course you will. Success principles are designed to achieve *maximum* success. Generosity is mandatory for maximum achievement. It stands to reason that if a person has their eye set on success, why not go all the way? To me, it makes no sense to travel down a path with the intention of not going all the way. "Go big or go home."

If you really think about it, we are all after financial security, a sense of accomplishment, and a healthy dose of contentment. If that is your state of mind, you won't have to lie whenever someone asks you how you are. "Awesome" is going to be your answer if you are already financially secure, content, and feeling accomplished. "Awesome" will be a more honest response than if those attributes were not in play.

We will all pass away at some point. When that time comes I think we should all have lived a life that is spent consciously focused on others, making the planet a better place. It's not that we're not important—we are—however, it's always better to experience life with others.

Consider an activity you participate in. I jog periodically. I don't really enjoy it, but it is good for me. What I do find is that running with others as a running group is 10 times better than running on your own. In a running group, you motivate each other by giving a bit of yourself to encourage others to complete the run. When we apply that attitude to all of our daily activities, we become the person assisting others on their journey, and receive their assistance in return.

Generosity is not the only success principle that will assist you; however, it is one of extreme significance. Your awesome life awaits, and as you read I hope you realize that now is the time. Having some wind in your sail, created by your genuine generous spirit, would be immensely helpful.

In a Nutshell

It's time for you to make your move: it's time to make that awesome life you have been dreaming about happen. Generosity is not mandatory in life; in fact, it's quite optional. Unfortunately, the vast majority of people never travel down the amazing path of generosity. Those that do realize the massive benefits to be had in contributing from their reservoir of talents and resources. In turn, they receive a blessing many times larger than what they contributed. That is The Law of Reciprocity.

It should be noted that your motive is crucial: those who give out of the goodness of their hearts will receive the benefits of The Law of Reciprocity. It is also true that those who give only to activate the principle or out of some sort of obligation will not receive this reward. I don't make up the rules, I just teach them!

This principle, like all other success principles, is like rowing a boat across a lake. Your strength will have a limit. You may not even reach the other side on your own. But if you implement the success principles, it will be like a gust of wind has filled your sail. You still have oars, but the wind will help propel you along.

It's correct to set goals, to desire to accomplish a lot while you are here. But it's a mistake to attempt to achieve all those goals by simply rowing. Generosity will fill your sail. Just steer the boat and enjoy the ride.

Helpful Exercise

Generosity is a major success principle. Therefore, being a generous person will fill our sail with an awesome wind and propel us to our desired destination. Let's do two things: first, let's acknowledge an area where we have been generous, contributing with the correct motive from our overabundance.

Secondly, let's itemize an opportunity where we could contribute to a person, organization, or function in a way that would be extremely helpful to someone else.

1) Where I am contributing right now _____

_____

_____

2) Where I have an opportunity to contribute _____

_____

_____

Remember your motives! Your contribution must come from a place driven by a genuine desire to help others.

We make a living by what we get, but we make a life by what we give.

Winston Churchill

Chapter Ten

LESS THINKING, MORE DOING

THIS BOOK IS about how it's time to get on with all your life's amazing aspirations. Of all the characteristics that create an obstacle to this amazing life, the tendency to overthink everything is a big one.

The vast majority of our coaching clients are realtors. Our job is to assist them to identify what they want in life. They are usually relatively clear on their business goals, and we in turn introduce them to the other aspects of their lives that make up a whole person. We discuss their spiritual position, physical health, mental wellbeing, and their relationships with family and friends. It's important that all aspects have clear goals and a defined path.

To achieve these goals, you might think that the most helpful actions would be to get up early, work hard every day, and complete your homework. Although our coaches do promote these ideas, by far the most helpful concept is the subject of this chapter: less thinking and more doing.

I am amazed at how much time is spent thinking and planning

in comparison to doing. Ready set, ready set, ready set ... at some point, we need to pull the trigger. A psychologist would call this "avoidance behaviour" (and just an FYI, when there is a name for a condition that means it's common).

If our subconscious mind is nervous about an activity, it will give us make-work projects to keep us busy. We end up continually preparing in order to avoid doing the actual activity. In most cases this occurs because the activity resides outside of our comfort zone. Therefore, we want to keep it a future event. We need to realize what is taking place in order to prevent it from becoming a cycle. Proper preparation is required, of course, but the sooner we can take action toward our goal the better off we are going to be in the long run.

I would even state that the occasional wrong decision is better than a constant life of indecision. Many people belabour decisions to the extent that few decisions are ever made. In that case, it's true that, over the course of their lives, they would have made fewer wrong decisions, but that's only because less is being accomplished in the first place!

Better to accidentally travel for a little while down the wrong path: you can always correct the mistake by retracing your steps. Make your adjustments from your starting point and then venture out in the correct direction. This will inevitably happen every now and again: life is full of big and small decisions. You can't live at the crossroads; you're not going to get much accomplished there.

In most cases, indecision is an ego problem. Not the egotistical problem—that's entirely something else. I'm talking about being overly concerned about making a mistake and being embarrassed or hurt. In this case, the issue is that you are protecting your ego. By doing so, you are effectively limiting yourself to life at the crossroads out of the simple fear of choosing the incorrect path.

I have made many wrong decisions in my life; it's more common for me than you might think. That is why I am certain that the benefits of making a decision, even if it is occasionally the wrong one, far outweigh continual inaction.

Although strategic planning is an important stage to success, it is exactly that: the planning stage. It should always be followed by implementation. The planning stage is designed to create a clear direction: to chart a path to our desired result. We are not supposed to stay in the planning stage. Things don't get done in the planning stage, they get planned. Things get done in the implementation stage, so that is where we must move to next.

People are excessively concerned about making mistakes. This traps them squarely in an inactive phase, in a state of limbo. Instead, they should make the decision to move forward. If it turns out to be the incorrect path, all is not lost—they simply have to turn around and venture back to their starting point.

Even incorrect decisions possess some value. In fact, we learn very little from the things we do correctly, but we learn a lot from our mistakes. Best to make a decision. If it's correct, then that's amazing: continue down that wonderful path. If you realize your decision is not working out, embrace your learning experience and return to your starting point all the wiser.

The magnitude of this concept is what allows some people to carry an amazing, lifelong dream all the way to their graves. It is a tragedy that they were so cautious about making a mistake, so concerned about being embarrassed or rejected, that they lived out their entire lives at the crossroads of that decision. It's a serious injustice. What's the worst that can happen? If it doesn't work out, we simply retrace our steps having learned a valuable life lesson.

Your awesome life awaits, and it's time for you to act on it. Do your due diligence: gather the correct amount of information and make your decision. You really can't lose. If the decision is correct—which it will be most of the time—that's awesome. If it isn't, learn your lesson and travel back to your starting point: no big deal.

Once you have the required information to make an informed decision, pull the trigger. Stop waiting for everything to be perfect. If you wait for everything to be perfect, you will spend your life in a state of indecision. Your finger will be on the trigger, but you'll never hear the bang. The people who spend all their days talking about what they are going to do are those that rarely accomplish anything.

I vividly remember having a meeting with a real estate broker in the fall of 2008 a few weeks after the opening of my company. In the meeting, the broker mentioned that what he really needed was an 8-week program to walk his realtors through their current training. My response was, "It sounds like our 8-week *Jumpstart* training program would be perfect." Fortunately for me, he didn't ask for too many details at that point. You see, we had plenty of programs planned, and we were more than capable of handling the training he required. But the truth is, we didn't have an 8-week training program called "Jumpstart." But we did when the program started 3 weeks later.

Making quick decisions and moving forward is the way to go. As it turns out, that 8-week "Jumpstart" training program became a staple for about 8 years.

As a self-assessment, think about how much you have planned and how often you venture out to accomplish your tasks, both physically and mentally. If you observe that you are a person who spends too much time in the planning stage and not enough time implementing your ideas, perhaps you should accept the fact that it's time. Act on your ideas to reach that awesome life that awaits you. Spend less time on the planning and more time on the doing.

If you think about a race car, before the race starts there is a lot of revving of the engine, adjusting this and that to prepare the vehicle. At some point, though, the race must take place; it wouldn't be much of a spectator sport if the race didn't actually take place. Your life is the same: of course preparation is required, but your life isn't going to be very exciting if you do not actually start living it.

For those involved in the race, it is the reason for the day: the preparation is just the beginning. It's the actual race that brings value. You can apply that same thinking to yourself. I don't think you would be very happy or content if you did not at some point run your race.

In a Nutshell

If we can accept that it's time to experience the awesome life that awaits us, we desperately need to think a lot less and do a lot more. Overthinking will effectively render us incapacitated. Our ability to move forward will be dramatically handicapped due to our excessive thinking about all the "what ifs".

Be a person that processes information quickly and follows it up with a firm, committed decision, including movement in that direction. It is true that occasionally you will select the incorrect route; when that happens, simply turn around and travel back to your starting point. Successful people make decisions and act on them. When they become aware that the decision is taking them in the wrong direction they are confident enough to accept their mistake and make the correction.

Avoid overthinking. It is better to occasionally make a decision that will require a change in route than to overthink everything for fear of a wrong decision. Your awesome life awaits you: it's just a few brave decisions away.

Helpful Exercise

Let's take a look and see if there is a decision (or decisions!) that you have been taking way too much time deliberating. Overthinking will stop you in your tracks. Perhaps you have been metaphorically revving up your engine when it's time to put it in gear and hit the gas pedal.

Overthinking Decision #1 _____

_____

Plan of Action: _____

_____

Overthinking Decision #2 _____

_____

Plan of Action: _____

_____

Overthinking Decision #3 _____

_____

Plan of action: _____

_____

If you make the wrong decision just correct it. At least it's done, which is better than living in a constant state of indecision.

Following through is the only thing that separates dreamers from people that accomplish great things.

Gene Hayden

Chapter Eleven

LIVE AWAY FROM THE EDGE

IN OUR QUEST to experience the bona fide awesome life that awaits us, living on the emotional edge is an immense stumbling block. In fact, this particular issue is often a major contributor to any mental slump you may experience. To correct it, we need to consciously move back from the edge and put guardrails in place that will prevent us from being future edge-dwellers.

A person living at the edge has effectively removed their margin for error: one wrong move and over they go. The slightest setback puts them over that edge. Logically, then, we want to dwell well away from that precipice, allowing for some movement either way that can occur without damaging consequences.

Let's take a look at some of the culprits that, when not kept in check, will leave us living on the edge.

Taking Everything Personally

I write and speak about this a lot. We have to realize that people will say many things, most of which is spoken without giving much thought to the potential repercussions. In fact, many such hurtful things are said by those lashing out from the edge they live at. We really need to learn to take things with a grain of salt.

Most comments are made absent of real belief or conviction. In many cases, they are probably comments from people you don't really like that much, anyway. They're on the edge themselves, so don't take their comments to heart. Just let it slide off you, and know in your heart that your reaction is not worth it.

Impatience

This common characteristic I don't understand: I'm not really sure what everyone is in a hurry for. I often say that none of us are getting out of this life alive, so what's the hurry? I say it jokingly but in truth, you get to live a certain number of days on this Earth and then it's off to the ever after. So why are we in such a hurry at this stage?

Most things take time. Relax and enjoy the process. Being an impatient person is like taking a cab directly to the very place you are supposed to avoiding: the emotional edge.

Life is amazing: relax and enjoy it. Some people are better-looking than others, some are born into money, and others experience a rags-to-riches story. Enjoy your lot in life, whatever it is. Know that impatience is a key contributor to mentally living on the edge.

Lack of Generosity

Generosity is an all-too-often missed piece of the puzzle. If you lack generosity, in addition to not being able to take advantage of the Law of Reciprocity, you will also be placed squarely on the edge. Remember what I said about how a hoarding mindset makes you more prone to stress and discontentment? It's because you are on the edge.

Our brain may try to rationalize how we can have more if we continually give of our resources, but it is not a concept that can be empirically broken down. As I repeatedly state, I don't make up the rules: I just teach them. And I can confidently say the more we contribute with a pure heart the more we receive. The reverse is also true: the less we contribute of our resources, the less we get back. Lack of contribution leaves us on the edge, and with no resources being reciprocated back to us, there is nothing to pull us away from it.

Keeping Up With the Joneses

As a very shallow attribute, no one ever wants to admit that they are obsessed with outwardly keeping up with the others around them. This common characteristic inevitably pushes a person to achieve the illusion of a status that does not match their reality. They will only be able to maintain this charade for so long before it all comes crashing down, and it is this that drives them to the edge.

The point of this book is to make you aware that it is time for the awesome life that *actually* awaits you, not the life you are pretending to live in this moment.

Spending a great deal of my business life as a realtor, I found it interesting how often I would list a home with a market value of, say, $500,000 when the owners still owed $450,000 on it. When I inquired how it was they came to owe so much on the property, their response was, "Well, my brother/sister/friend has a big house..." That is not a reason to over-extend!

I also noticed how stressed these people were. That would certainly be a result of living the last number of years under financial stress, driving themselves to the edge just to keep up with the Joneses.

Your life is amazing. So live it on your terms: keep your eyes off others. It could be that they're the ones trying to keep up with you!

Pursuing the Path You Know to Be Wrong

I did say earlier that it's better to occasionally make a wrong decision than to live in indecision. Once you have made a committed decision, if it turns out to be incorrect, then I have no issue with making adjustments. But when you realize a path is wrong and you continue to pursue it anyway, or if you are aware from the beginning that this path is incorrect for you, it will lead you to the dangerous edge.

For instance, if you are aware from the very beginning that this route compromises your integrity, yet you follow whatever about it that entices you, you will end up on the edge. Or if you know in the beginning that this path is not the right choice for you, your destination will undoubtedly be the edge.

For someone else this path may be fine: they don't necessarily carry your set of values, or they may be seeking something different than you are. The truth is it's wrong for you, and you knowingly followed it anyway. Don't go—it leads to the edge!

Unhappy With Who You Are

This is a tough one. If, after reading helpful writings such as mine, you still consider yourself inadequate or your contributions insignificant, you probably need to speak to someone who can provide you with the bona fide assistance you need to discover just how awesome you actually are.

Everyone has massive amounts to contribute. Some may seem more valuable than others, but in reality all are significant. Refusing to acknowledge the value of what you bring to the table of life has the potential to bring on feelings of worthlessness.

To avoid this, I recommend you make a list of all your positive attributes and purposefully look at it every day. Search for opportunities to share those attributes with others. Maybe you are great listener, and to you that doesn't seem significant. However, it very much is important to the person who needs to share a burden with someone.

Being unhappy with who you are is a great way to live at 123 Edge Way. You are an amazing person. I know that, because everyone is an amazing person. And seeing as you are part of "everyone," this means you: you are amazing.

Lack of Mental Breaks

This is another topic I find myself talking about a lot in seminars. I am a little concerned with the pace people run themselves at in this day and age. We, as humans, require down time: moments to mentally exhale. Although I'm a big believer in technology and how it can easily contribute to growth, I also recognize that it's a main contributor to the removal of down time. Everywhere I go I see people on their phones. In fact, many times others have seen me scrolling through emails or sending texts when I should be taking a break.

Technology is convenient and necessary, but I recommend you allow your body to live the way it was designed: to work hard and be productive with frequent mental exhales. Scrolling through your phone is not an exhale, especially if you are the person who constantly wants to know what everyone thinks about your latest comment, post, or opinion.

That is not an exhale; in fact, it's quite the opposite. You get all worked up about something that, in all likelihood, has very little to do with you. Your brain is, in essence, running to the edge. Don't get me wrong: there are times to speak up, just not at the level that some take it to. If that's you, you are purposefully being an edge dweller.

You might be wondering: what does a mental exhale look like? Go for a walk to enjoy your natural surroundings, go for dinner and leave your phone in the car, read, or watch a movie uninterrupted.

The other day at a seminar I was teaching this very topic. It's interesting to read the crowd's body language when they realize that they don't give themselves these mental exhales. A few came to me afterward and said it would be impossible for them to be away from their phone because they might miss something. I find that sad. Being so anxious that you might miss something by being away from your phone for such a short time—that kind of talk can only happen from the edge. If this is you, you'd best be careful you don't fall over!

Lack of Grounding

For me, I like to go to church—that keeps me grounded on many different levels. Others may experience the same type of grounding at their place of faith. If you don't lean toward the spiritual, then you may find that traditions can bring stability to you. Some non-spiritual activities such as Saturday morning pancake breakfasts, volunteering regularly at a soup kitchen, or Friday night pizza and a movie, can all bring some grounding to you and your family. The more wholesome traditions you commit to, the more grounded you will be.

My wife Coleen and I make it a habit to always walk to dinner on Friday night if we are in town. Even in the winter, we bundle up and venture out. There literally aren't any eateries within walking distance from our home that we have not walked to.

Good traditions will keep you grounded, leaving a nice gap between you and the edge.

Too Much Passion for Something You Don't Really Care About

This one confuses me. I realize that we live in an instant society where everyone has the ability to provide their opinion almost instantaneously. I'm a big advocate for speaking up about situations you are passionate about. When there is something that you simply cannot stop thinking about, and you possess a constructive opinion on the matter, then I think it is your responsibility to speak and have your opinion heard.

However, I regularly observe individuals who, in all honesty haven't even been aware of a particular situation before that very moment, instantly reach a level of passion that has them touring dangerously close to the edge.

When we become passionate about an issue, we open ourselves up to the danger of treading too close to the edge: that's the risk of passion. When you are genuinely passionate about something, the risk is worth it. But why go there over the edge for something that does not truly resonate with you? Save your passion for things you genuinely care about.

Although there are many other characteristics that can accidently move us toward the edge, I think you get my point: positive behaviour tends to move us to a safe, secure place, while negative behaviour consigns us to becoming an edge-dweller. From there, all it will take is just one bad day and over we go.

When we live at the edge for an extended time, we have a tendency to say and do many things that we come to regret at a later date. The edge is a stressful place, so it's unrealistic to expect ourselves to act reasonably while experiencing that kind of daily pressure. On the other hand, when we dwell a comfortable distance from the drop-off, our heads will be in a better place that allows us to make more calculated statements and decisions.

Let's take a look at some things we can do to better position our lives a comfortable distance from the danger zone.

Count Your Blessings

This exercise will quickly uncover the magnitude of how amazing your current life really is. Once you start, the list just keeps going and going: it's really quite an enlightening process to recognize just how much is going your way at this very point in time.

The other day I issued this exercise to a client who was dealing with some setbacks in both life and business, which happens to all of us on occasion. I received a text from her about 15 minutes later saying, "Thank you, I'm over it." In our next conversation she mentioned that once she started identifying her blessings, she filled up several pages. Her current issues were still present, but the real difference was her perspective on how she viewed those items. She told me, "Although they are real and do require my attention, they are not as overwhelming as I previously thought."

The issues will pass, but the blessings remain. Count your blessings!

When One Door Closes Another Opens

This principle often puzzles me with its reliability: when one opportunity ends or falls through, it will be shortly followed by a new opportunity: a new open door. I am experiencing this issue as we speak. Yesterday, a door closed for me. I now have a choice: to mope around or actively look for a new door, the one that is probably already slightly ajar. I think you can guess that my plan is to be on the lookout for that new door and have a peek inside.

Although this principle is a life truth, most people will spend their time lamenting the lost opportunity and never see the light shining through the crack in the next door. Keep moving: behind the next door is an exciting opportunity.

Acknowledge Your Accomplishments

When you do something that you know is an accomplishment— of any size, mind you—make sure that does not go internally unacknowledged. I'm not saying you should brag about all your conquests: a compliment is only a compliment when someone else gives it to you! I'm saying that you should regularly make a mental note and acknowledge what you have achieved. Accomplishments can be drawn upon in times of future struggle or challenge—provided you remember to reflect often!

The object is to make yourself more resilient to life's oh-so-common obstacles. Obviously if you lack a reservoir of past accomplishments, it will render you vulnerable to overreacting to every passing challenge.

You do many amazing things, so take internal note of them. It will probably come in handy in the not-too-distant future.

Be a Person Others Can Count On

This will require some sacrifice on your part; however, the satisfaction to be gained by being a person others know they can depend upon is immense.

I realize that being a dependable person is not always convenient: perhaps after a long day all you want to do is put your feet up and rest. But you have a friend who needs assistance moving a couch. As a dependable person, you take a breath and gladly help out, keeping your desire to rest to yourself.

If you look around at your sphere of family and friends, you will become quite aware of who around you can be relied upon, and who are less reliable. The question is, which group do you fit into? Being a person others can rely upon is a massive character builder. Be that person!

Get Over Things Quickly

I literally cannot stop talking about this point: it comes up in every book I write and every seminar I teach. At the end of the day, holding onto negative things will suck out all our energy, enthusiasm, and aspirations, rendering us lazy and uninspired. If this is you, this book is your wakeup call: your awesome life awaits you. So it's time to quickly get over the things that are holding you back.

If you think about the things you hold onto, are they really that big of a deal? If the answer is yes then fine; however, if the answer is no, then let them go. There are doors out there sitting slightly ajar for you, waiting to be kicked wide open! It's either that or mope around: the decision is entirely up to you. Life is short, so don't hold onto things: it's not worth it!

Do Something Every Day for Someone Else

A strong sense of character is required for you to move into that awesome life that awaits you. Doing something that is solely for the sake of someone else, no strings attached, is a massive character-builder. Seeing as it's something you should do every day, this contribution is mostly going to be on the smaller side of the equation. For instance, maybe in the office a colleague mentions they need to get something from the stockroom. You pipe in, "You know what, I need a stretch. Let me get that for you," and away you go.

Maybe you decide to buy a random person coffee (that's my personal favourite). Perhaps as you manoeuvre your shopping cart to your car, you stop and assist someone else in the loading of their groceries. I realize it's a small thing, but built up over time it's a huge character-builder, and we could all use more of that.

Work to Understand Others

This particular goal will test your patience and stretch you as a person. We have been conditioned to be outspoken regarding our own opinions and beliefs, but it's time to consider others for a change. Most of us could do a better job at purposefully opening our minds to what others hold as core values. I am certainly not suggesting we compromise our positions, I'm just saying that taking the steps to understand how others feel and why they feel that way can go a long way toward constructive conversation.

Your choices are to be a person who is firm in your views but keeps an open mind, or to be one who is seen as continually argumentative. The combative choice leads to a closed-down mindset, not conducive to personal growth. Choose to be a person who works to understand others: this will lead to your success. As an added bonus, it prevents you from having to argue your point of view with everyone you encounter.

Think Before You Speak

Another handy idea is to think before we respond to what others say. Trust me: this will take some practice. Think about how many things you have said that, in hindsight, you regret. Because once you say something, you cannot unsay it. You can apologize, and somewhat correct the statement, but you will still likely be left wishing you had held your peace.

Personally, I am not a passive person: I do possess strong opinions and beliefs. However, I work hard to pick my spots. Even so, I admit that I have made comments that, in hindsight, I wish I had showed more restraint in speaking.

Before you judge me too harshly, if you are honest with yourself you will see that I have a lot of company, including you. We cannot do anything about past indiscretions, but we can and should be more careful with our potentially hurtful comments in the future. Your opinion counts, but it should be noted that it is not always correct. A sharp tongue is a pathway to the edge: think before you speak.

When implementing these attributes to facilitate personal growth, we are elevating other people on a daily basis. It's not that you are not important—of course you are. However, other people also occupy the planet. It's imperative that we show respect and acknowledge what they bring to the table, as they are valuable contributors in their own right.

Living too close to the edge, whether mentally or emotionally, will rob us of our desired personal growth. Implementing these points effectively will move us to a safe, secure location away from the edge.

There are many people in your social sphere who count on you, and the truth is, you are not much help to them while you reside close to the edge. All of your positive qualities, characteristics, and attributes are rendered moot.

The truth is, when you are on the edge you are solely focussed on yourself—and for good reason! If you are not paying attention to everything you do, you may metaphorically topple over. You really have no choice but to focus totally on maintaining your own balance. Therefore, the trend in your focus will inevitably be drawn inward. Those around you who are in need of your support are going to have to wait: you currently have your hands full not toppling off an edge, one that doesn't come with a parachute.

If we can successfully implement the principles in this chapter and avoid the common pitfalls, we can put ourselves in a position to supply the necessary support to those around us. This, in turn, makes us a better friend, colleague, parent, or partner. The edge is a very bad place to live: it's not even a fun place to visit. Do yourself a favour, and don't go there.

If you consider life on the edge versus life when lived a safe distance back, the differences are astounding. At the edge, it's all self-focussed as you balance with the occasional foot dangling over. In this state, you are truthfully not much assistance to anyone.

On the other hand, a life that observes the physical and emotional edge from a safe distance is one that is calm and content. Note I used the word "content" not "complacent": content is being comfortable and calm, while complacency is a lazy attitude. Content is what you want; complacency is probably the topic of a whole other book I could write.

When someone else needs assistance, the calm and content

person is gladly there to offer whatever they need. Meanwhile, the edge-dweller usually responds with, "I would love to help, but I'm kind of slammed right now," since they have to be totally focussed on themselves.

You have a choice of which person you will be: calm, content, and confused by those folks you see off in the distance who are struggling at the edge, or actually one of those people struggling. The awesome life that awaits you can't happen if you are an edge-dweller.

Whatever you think about expands in your mind and in turn gains its own identity. Gentle contentment breeds the continuation of a calm and content manner. Scattered thoughts and a struggling mindset create scattered actions and further struggles. "When it rains it pours" is the mantra of edge dwellers.

I realize you are reading this book because you have a desire to better yourself: to once and for all extend yourself to the level of success that you have dreamed about. In the clients that hire us to coach them, I can clearly see they are at their wits' end. Something has to dramatically change. In many cases, they have only come to us at an "enough is enough" moment. I remind them that they didn't have to wait until they were desperate to get some help. Then we go about moving them away from the edge.

Challenge yourself. Know where you put your values: what you hold in your heart as right and wrong. Take stock of what is really important to you and what is, for lack of a better term, artificially important.

When we hold in our hearts our morally-significant ideals, it would be difficult to get to the edge even if we tried. On the other hand, when we mentally invest in immoral values, it is like the edge is a magnet and we are iron. The more improper values we adopt, the stronger the magnetic pull. As such, a series of incorrect decisions will inevitably draw us to exactly where we don't want to go.

The truth is, you inherently know good values from harmful ones. The good ones lead you to comfort and contentment. You should also be aware that incorrect values lead to the edge. When an improper value or decision presents itself, the fact that no one will ever know or get hurt is not a reason to choose it. Someone will get hurt: you.

My job at Rob Vivian Coaching is to assist individuals in achieving their dreams and desires. To accomplish the awesome life that awaits them, my first job is to move them away from the edge. We must relocate them to a safe place where calm and contentment reside: a place where they will once again be in the position to affect others in a positive fashion.

It's common for my efforts to be met with some apprehension. I consider this reasonable: after all, edge-dwelling can become a habit, if not a lifestyle. Sometimes, it takes a while for the client to understand that the goal they are aiming for is not launched from the edge. The launch pad is actually set safely back, in a secure location where we can ensure everything is in order prior to initiating the launch sequence.

It's not uncommon for it to take some time to exchange the hectic, on-edge lifestyle for a calm, content life. But once that has been accomplished, you are mentally prepared to locate your own launch pad for a massive step forward. Or you can live in a stressful existence on the edge; it's entirely your call.

In a Nutshell

Living on the edge, whether mentally or emotionally, will render us incapable of pushing forward to the amazing experience of upward personal growth. The edge is a hectic, stressful place, filled only with more of the same.

In order to experience the awesome life that awaits us, we must first realize that any major leaps cannot happen at the edge. We must instead move away to a calmer, more stable environment in order to be physically and mentally prepared for our upward growth.

The edge is nothing more than continual stress. It's not a place where dreams come true. Don't live there!

Helpful Exercise

I hope I no longer have to sell you on the fact that the edge is a bad place to spend your time. Therefore, let's do a little exercise. Be honest and itemize a couple areas where you have inadvertently strayed a little too close to the edge. Use my categories in this chapter to identify what bad, on-edge habits you may be forming. Once you start paying attention to it, you'll find that everything within you is screaming at you to let this thing go and migrate to a safer zone.

Edge Habit #1: _____

Solution: _____

_____

Edge Habit #2: _____

Solution: _____

_____

Edge Habit #3: _____

Solution: _____

_____

I know you want to improve yourself—it's the correct thing to want.
Unfortunately, growth does not take place at the edge.
All you can do there is try not to fall over!

If someone can easily topple you, it's because you are too close to the edge. That's a you thing.

Rob Vivian

Chapter Twelve

TOUGHEN UP A BIT

I ADMIRE THAT you are taking steps to improve your life. I hope that, having read this far, you have picked up on the importance of continual improvement in all the aspects of your life. It's crucial that we ward off the feeling of "This is it: I have arrived."Think about it! What is life for after you have decided that you have accomplished everything on your path? What are you going to do then? Are you going to sit around and watch TV, or continually read news articles on your phone? Truth is, that is exactly what most people do.

I would argue that you are only done when your life is done: it's never too late. There is always a goal to be set, something in your life to improve. Perhaps you retire at 65 years of age, having spent a positive life on the accumulation of assets. You now have a comfortable financial retirement of travel, entertainment, and enjoyment ahead of you.

Although that is true, you still should not sit around and do nothing. Perhaps you can work on being in the best shape of your life, learn a new language, or volunteer at a worthwhile charity. We are not designed to sit around and wait to die: that is just purely lazy. Stay active, both physically and mentally, until you are done. Even if you are in your retirement, it's still time: your awesome life awaits.

In order to physically and mentally live in that constant, uplifting state of your life being about perpetual growth, you are going to need to be a little tougher.

Things will not always go your way. Sometimes when we're thinking negatively, we mistakenly believe that others have a smoother ride to success. And although I guess that is possible, in all likelihood it's probably not factual. Sometimes our "woe is me" attitude can distort the facts. The truth is, the others that you perceive as experiencing a smoother ride are likely just great actors or actresses. They are quite possibly observing what they assess as your smooth journey through life.

I encounter many people in my seminars: mixing with negative attitudes is a common occurrence for me. When I share that we need to toughen up a little in order to add fuel to our journey, some people spin these empowering thoughts in a negative fashion. They say, "Wait a minute—are you saying that I need to work to improve myself until the day I die? That I should have no time to sit around and do nothing?"

"Yes," I emphatically respond. "Isn't that exciting? You can, and should, experience personal growth your entire life. You will avoid being in a position where your personal contribution has ceased to exist. How exciting is that?"

Sad to say, sometimes people are not ready to change their view on the world so drastically. In which case they walk away disappointed, believing I'm a little crazy.

Sometimes the light does come on for them, and I have played a small part in directing that individual down a more successful path. Even in the scenario where we part ways and they believe me a lunatic, there is still some value in our conversation. Although I was not the person to open their eyes to a better and bigger life, I did plant a seed. Perhaps in the future someone who brings a similar message will water that subconscious, fragile thought, and it will bloom into a realization.

If you can embrace the idea that life is designed to be lived as a continual upward projection until the day you take your last breath, everything will change for you. You will realize that we all have something in common: we are all trying to get somewhere on our personal highway of life.

Many things will happen for you and me along the way. Plenty of them will be positive. Others will be perceived by us as negative at the time. In hindsight, often those events that appeared to be negative will have actually served us well. I could literally write a book on the scenarios that present themselves initially as negative and then play out to be a massive positive influence. I myself have had many experiences that would fit into this category. If I were a gambling man, I would be willing to bet that you could say the same.

When a benefit arrives disguised as a detriment, we will in all likelihood not recognize the fortune it could afford us until we move past it and view it from the other side. This is where the idea to toughen up a bit comes into play: if we are mentally weak, it is quite conceivable that we may not conquer this obstacle. In that case, we may never have the luxury to view this scenario from the opposite side, and the ultimate benefit may go permanently undiscovered.

Momentum is an amazing thing. We constantly experience it as either an upward or downward spiral. A main contributing factor to the direction of our spiral is how well we deal with adversity: are we tough, or are we fragile? This is all about attitude. I confess that early in my life I would fall on the wrong side of this equation: I took criticism too much to heart, hindering my ability to get past what I viewed as negative situations. I did not allow myself the luxury of reviewing the event from the other side so that the ultimate benefit could reveal itself.

Over time, I have vastly improved this area of my life; in fact, now it's a strength of mine. For some, possessing mental strength is a natural attribute they were born with. Others, like me, are required to obtain the mental toughness through learned practice. So let's purposefully exercise this required mental toughness and quickly put your latest obstacle squarely in the rear view mirror.

One of the amazing by-products of being mentally tough is courage, which is quite the attribute to possess. I don't mean action-hero courage: I'm not suggesting you turn into James Bond. I mean quiet, daily courage. The kind of courage that is required to speak up when the time is right, to carry yourself with confidence, and to walk into a room without feeling insecure. It is an attribute that everyone around you has no choice but to take notice of when you are in the room.

Courage is a by-product of making a conscious decision to toughening up. Another excellent attribute that finds its way into your makeup is that you become a person who is self-possessed and not easily offended.

It's been said that we build a firm foundation with the bricks that others throw in our direction. It is because of this that I'm a little concerned with the modern thought process that leads to people becoming offended every time a metaphorical brick is tossed in their direction. What happened to "sticks and stones will break my bones, but words will never hurt me"?

A healthier tactic is to take the metaphorical brick for what it's worth, considering both the source and the topic. If you determine that the accusation is totally off-base, dispose of it and use it to fortify your foundation. After all, firm foundations do require bricks.

The problem, in my humble opinion, is the ever-increasing tendency for people to become offended by everything they disagree with. This creates a foundation that lacks in both resilience and durability.

Unfortunately, the natural progression is illustrated by how quickly our world goes from offended to outraged. Think about how often you hear the word "outrage." For me, I would say it's daily. Someone makes a statement, one that they threw out as a casual comment, and immediately social media is all abuzz with "outrage."

In days gone by, when a person made a comment that others found offensive, it was possible that, over time, the feeling of offence could transition from offence to outrage. That middle step, the addition of time, seems to have been eliminated in today's society. We move from disagreement to outrage in a matter of minutes.

This new method of human interaction leaves us in a dangerous situation. A person living in a perpetual state of outrage will hinder the pursuit of their own dreams by spending too much time in that unproductive mindset.

Please don't misunderstand me: I realize comments can be made that will cut someone to the core. Sometimes those bricks are way over the top and hit where they hurt.

But being offended by everything that does not fit your own opinions, and quickly moving that offence to outrage is a very unhealthy way to live. You rob yourself of an opportunity to consider the source of that brick, take it for what it's worth, and use it to fortify your foundation.

Now that we have had this discussion, pay attention to the information you receive on a daily basis. The next time someone makes a comment that you consider to be a little off-base, ask yourself: is outrage really the correct response here? Or could that brick be put to better use securing my personal foundation?

It will be difficult to realize that it's time to achieve the awesome life that awaits you if you spend your days living in a state of outrage. Are there times to be outraged? Yes, of course: just not at every third story on the newsfeed on your phone. Everyone tosses bricks, and everyone receives bricks. Let's put them to good use instead of spending our days being outraged about things that, in the big picture, really don't matter.

Our past influences our present. Positive results are achieved from a positive mindset. And because every coin has two sides, a negative mindset in turn fosters negative results. I think it's self-explanatory that living in an outraged state of mind will yield more of the same. Life has enough obstacles. It doesn't make sense to create more by allowing your brain to quickly escalate to outrage when you disagree with someone's opinion or position.

If it's not directed at you, leave it alone; if it is directed at you, catch that brick, consider its source, and use it to fortify your base. Don't join the outrage club.

If you think about it, there are all sorts of opinions around you that you agree with, and an equal multitude that are not your personal viewpoint. That's life: accept the good and the bad. You will be exposed to all these opinions along your path. If you like it that way, that's both convenient and awesome. If it's not your way of looking at things, 99% of the time you should let it go and move along.

It's time for the awesome life that awaits you, and that means it's time to move forward. Toughen up a bit and achieve those amazing, worthwhile goals you have set for you and your family. I shouldn't have to point out that constantly being outraged about others' opinions is not a flattering quality.

Think about your own family tree: you probably have quite the cast of characters. For me, there are some family members I should be spending more time with, and others that a couple times a year is just about right. However, they are my family, and I take the good with the bad. The onus is on me to be accepting; it's not important to me that everyone agrees with my viewpoints.

I suppose if everyone thought like me that would be very convenient—for me. However, that is not the planet I live on, nor is it yours. It's important that we pursue a mindset that supports personal growth, putting ourselves in a position to achieve the life we aspire to. Being accepting and understanding are great starts; being outraged all the time is not.

Our level of disdain toward someone who has, in our mind, wronged us will be directly proportional to our internal toughness. The more fragile we are, the greater our reaction to the situation will be. On the other hand, the tougher we are the less of an impact the intrusion will have.

If you find yourself giving way too much credence to all the perceived injustices you experience, you might want to look yourself in the mirror and ask a blatantly honest question: is my continual overreaction to what I perceive as not going my way a result of me simply not being mentally tough enough to deal with life's natural ebb and flow?

If we are going to be 100% honest with ourselves, this could be a difficult question to answer; however, answered correctly, it could be a first step to a much bigger world.

I know we all have a strong desire to be the person that others can count on, whom they can go to in times of turmoil. We want to be the stabilizing force for those around us, what others may refer to as their "rock." That is going to be difficult if we are too easily offended by those around us, living in a continually hurt state.

I realize that there will be times in which our proper reaction to an offence is one of deep hurt. It would be wise to allocate our deeply hurt feelings for those rare times where this emotion applies.

The truth is, people will often allow situations to affect them that, in all honesty, are not of the magnitude to inflict the deep emotional hurt they are experiencing. In most cases I feel that a simple state of annoyance would be a much more appropriate state of mind.

I don't want to be the person who is constantly saying, "I think you might be overreacting here," but I do believe that being annoyed or disappointed with an infraction is more suitable than getting emotionally worked up.

When we allow our inner emotions to travel to a dark place every time something doesn't go our way, we remove our ability to offer support and comfort to others. Take things in stride: when negative situations occur, ensure your inner self reacts at an appropriate level. Being too easily offended does not serve those around you well.

Note I didn't say "if" things happen. Things will definitely happen, and that's good news—that's how you know you are a participant in the game of life. Mentally tough people possess a "never give up" attitude. You were not designed to fold up like a cheap tent every time adversity comes your way. "When the going gets tough the tough get going." I love that saying, although it's harder to live than it sounds. However, it is still a truth.

We need to make a decision: either to be mentally tough—where our belief system is one of perseverance, focus, and determination—or to live our lives continually upset about the things that, in the big picture, don't really matter. On the tough side are our leaders, while on the weak side are the sensationalists. Choose leader!

In a Nutshell

Walking down that path to the awesome life that awaits you is going to require you to move in a different direction than the masses. If you find yourself following with common thinking, you might want to stop and assess your position. The tendency is to speak up as soon as you disagree with something that has been said. These days, most people skip the "upset" stage and move directly to "outrage." If you have a bona fide desire to move forward in all the aspects of your life, your states of outrage should be few and far between.

Let's toughen up a little bit. When an infraction presents itself, consider the source. Apply the proper emotion to it: you should be annoyed and disappointed far more often than outraged.

Remember: you are not wearing a Velcro suit. Not everything has to stick. It's going to be difficult to get to where you want to be if you allow yourself to be an adhesive for life's challenges. Life's too short. Break up the outrage club!

Helpful Exercise

I am aware of the traps that will be set in your way as stumbling blocks. It's not really about not having them: they are part of life. In many cases, they are required to give you the necessary strength to complete your mission. The trick is to manage them correctly when they present themselves.

When things come to your attention and you strongly disagree, a counterattack takes your brain into an unproductive zone. Rather than immediately overreacting, why not ask yourself a couple of simple questions.

1) Does this really affect my life?
2) Is this really a big deal?
3) Am I really involved in this situation?

If you answer "no" to any of these, then, toughening up a little may be the appropriate move. List a couple areas where you are acutely aware that you are taking things a little too personally.

Situation #1 to Toughen Up and Get Over _____

_____

_____

Situation #2 to Toughen Up and Get Over _____

_____

_____

Situation #3 to Toughen Up and Get Over _____

_____

_____

Allowing yourself to be continually bogged down with the little issues will create a massive roadblock. In essence, you will be preventing yourself from achieving your goals, desires, and dreams.

Toughen up a little and get out of your own way!

Amateurs sit and wait for inspiration,
the rest of us just get up and go to work.

Stephen King

Chapter Thirteen

HAVING MONEY INSTEAD OF MONEY HAVING YOU

OF COURSE I want you to have money; money is a part of the awesome life that awaits you. I don't think you would feel like life is operating at a higher level if you are continually short on revenue. The question to ask yourself is, do you have money or does money have you? "Semantics," you might say. However, I'm here to tell you otherwise.

Without question, money is required to live at that higher level of awesome living that you seek. I often say that you should set a goal to eliminate financial stress from your personal life. Living every day with financial stress is a circumstance you should work hard to avoid. Life has enough built-in stress already; adding financial burdens will only serve to push a person over the edge. It can exaggerate a person's negative circumstances to create more undue stress.

When financial stress is not a part of our daily living situation, we are free to handle life's natural flow as it is presented to us. Our current financial circumstances will not magnify the issues we encounter.

Inhabiting a desire to possess money is natural. It's going to be difficult to supply for your family and be a positive impact on others without financial resources. Therefore, there is nothing wrong with pushing yourself in the direction of monetary gain; I have been doing it my whole life. The important thing is to keep the level of importance that you allow money to play in check.

Money isn't the be all and end all. We hear a lot about balance, and as a seminar speaker I speak about it often. If you really think about all the aspects of your life, money is the least important—and rightly should be. It may appear, due to circumstances, that money is the thing you need the most right now, but in the big picture it's not as important.

If you had to choose between money or your health, which would you choose? How about money or your family? Money always falls to the lesser priority.

There will be times that you desperately need money. In those instances, it is all too common to make the mistake of elevating money to a higher position on the list of personal aspects than it deserves. When this happens, you become out of balance. Everything may look fine on the outside, but on the inside your calm has temporarily escaped you to be replaced with stress.

Therefore, when accumulating financial holdings, you must place your desire for money in its correct position within the list of life's aspects. So even though it is a goal, it shouldn't be the most important goal for you to achieve.

I want you to have ample financial resources; I really do. I am also acutely aware of the pitfalls we all too often fall into. These pitfalls only block us from accumulating financial assets.

Most people have carried mental blockages about money from their childhood into their adult life. Our parents, although meaning well, accidently imprinted negative views about money into our subconscious minds. Their intention was not to create a limiting belief, but it has since been processed incorrectly in our brain. I'm sure you have heard these statements before:

1) Money does not grow on trees
2) They might be rich, but are they happy?
3) Money can't buy happiness—or friends
4) Money is the root of all evil
5) What am I, an ATM?

In comparison, take a few minutes to write down all the positive statements that you heard about money while you were growing up.

Don't feel bad if you couldn't come up with any: I couldn't. Most adults carry these limiting beliefs into adulthood, subconsciously blocking their ability to attain a comfortable or above-average income. When the subconscious mind believes that money is bad, it will keep the "bad" money away from you. So even in your best efforts to obtain wealth, you will be in your own way.

Let's take a look at these over-prevalent statements:

Money Does Not Grow on Trees

Of course it doesn't. However, holding onto this particular limiting belief will create a subconscious scarcity mindset. This is the opposite of the more desired idea of abundance.

They Might Be Rich, but Are They Happy?

That depends: are they rich while keeping money in its correct perspective? Are they valuing all other aspects of their lives ahead of money? If yes, then they will be happy and balanced.

On the other hand, if they have chased the almighty dollar and elevated money past life's more important aspects, then the answer will probably be no; they will likely not be happy. They'll have lots of abundance and no one to share it with. Those who should have been cherished along the way are probably long gone.

Money Can't Buy Happiness—or Friends

It's true that money cannot make people like you, nor can it make you genuinely happy. It should be noted that if you are a person who keeps money in its proper place, it makes room for the more important aspects of your life to take precedence.

Therefore, true happiness will be achieved not because of your wealth, but because of your balance. Human nature is such that those who have their priorities straight are the people others enjoy associating with. This, in turn, creates lasting, meaningful relationships.

Money Is the Root of All Evil

"Money is the root of all evil" is a misquote from 1 Timothy 6:10, where there is one crucial piece missing. The scripture is "For the love of money is the root of all kinds of evil." What the scripture is saying here is exactly what we are discussing in this chapter.

When we love money, we elevate it from its designated position of the least important of life's aspects. For instance, perhaps an individual has allocated money as their most important aspect. That person is way out of balance and heading for a whole lot of bad, or "the root of all evil."

What Am I, an ATM?

This one is interesting. On the one hand, we do want to teach our children that money is something to be respected and not necessarily easily accessible at every turn. On the other, we do not want to imprint into their subconscious minds that money is difficult to attain.

Instead of using this particular phrase, perhaps a better approach would be to say, "That item is not necessary right now," or "Let's commit to experiencing that in the future."

I realize children ask for a lot, and at times we are simply mentally preoccupied, which often results in an answer that probably won't serve them well in their adult life. No one is perfect. We won't create a limiting belief from an occasional inadvertent statement; however, continual ones will subconsciously affect the minds of those we love and wish well.

Here are some healthy statements about money that are much better in the long run:

1) Money is a very useful tool
2) I am very generous with my money
3) Money does open up some options
4) With money, patience is key
5) You can have it all; you just can't have it all at once
6) Money comes to me
7) I continually have more money than I require

With its natural flow, life has enough ups and downs. Experiencing money issues will only further complicate circumstances. Therefore, it's important that we think correctly about money, especially when speaking to our children.

Deep in our hearts, we would love to be that person who helps others with their financial needs when an unfortunate circumstance presents itself. Unfortunately, most people are relegated to feeling bad while they watch from the sidelines because of their own (possibly secret) financial issues. Once you realize that it's time for you to reach the awesome life that awaits you, you can put yourself in a position to step up and be that person who can be relied upon.

It's been said that we are supposed to leave the planet a better place than we found it. Although there are many ways to accomplish this feat, being a person's temporary financial rescue would be one.

I would imagine that if you are not in a position to assist others at this point, your goal is to work toward making financial security your reality. In turn, you allow yourself to become the person your heart has desired your entire life. As you implement the essence of these writings, your life will improve on all levels: increased financial revenues are also part of the process.

In the beginning, you will probably need to clean up some of your own debt—the debt people often pretend they don't have. It's also natural to spoil yourself a bit: perhaps some travel, new clothes, maybe even a new vehicle. It's all part of the process. Don't feel bad; it's how life works. It's normal to give yourself some financial love prior to being another's financial assistant.

Money is not meant to be hoarded; it's meant to be used wisely. Notice you never see a hearse pulling a U-Haul: you can't take it with you. Just as it's not to be hoarded, money is not meant to be squandered: it's a bit of a balancing act. Expect financial resources to come your way, supply for yourself and your family, and then be helpful to others who are not as fortunate as you.

Money really is an amazing thing in our modern world: lack of it limits your options and acts as a ball and chain. But, given that every coin has two sides, increased money opens up options everywhere and creates mental freedom. When you have a surplus, you will have eliminated financial stress; a shortage, and you will lie awake at night in secret agony.

If you exchange negative viewpoints about money for healthy ones, your financial situation will not change overnight. However, it will definitely change. This is because you become what you think about. This principle is the number one thing that guides your life in a positive or negative direction: it is whichever direction you choose.

A more positive viewpoint about money will take you down a path of personal prosperity. It might take some time, but at least you are on the correct path: a path to a much bigger life. Which is, after all, why you are reading this book.

If you work out today you will not be ripped today. But if you work out on a regular basis, eventually you will be. On the other hand, if you eat fast food every day, you won't be fat today, but it will be your eventual outcome. Think positively about money and travel in a positive financial direction.

Some tips that I find help when thinking about money:

Live Within Your Means

It's important that we live an amazing life within our financial means. Yes, maybe a friend has a more impressive home or car. And maybe they can afford it, and maybe they can't. Perhaps they are simply "keeping up" with someone else; perhaps that someone else is you! It's important that your personal existence takes place within your realm of possibility.

Does it really matter if your home is 1,500 square feet instead of the 2,800-square-foot home a friend has? A home is where your children do their homework, where everyone finds refuge from a sometimes busy and stressful world: a home is a home. If it is within your ability to own a larger one, then great: that's awesome.

Spending a lot of my adult life as a realtor, I did notice that every time the market took a downturn thousands would lose their houses. Obviously, a lot of people were not adhering to the principle of living within their means. Unfortunately, although in our hearts we possess a desire to assist others, we may find ourselves secretly in the same boat, thus hindering our ability to be the assistance we would love to be. In fact, we might be one bad break away from being that person in need of assistance.

If you live above your means, I'm here to inform you that this will not end well for you. You might want to ask yourself: who it is that you are trying to impress?

Have Multiple Accounts with Smaller Balances

As an example, let's say you have an extra $25,000 right now in a savings account. It may tempt you to make a purchase that is not really necessary. With the one account, it is easy to look at the $25,000 and rationalize the viability of the purchase.

On the other hand, let's say that same $25,000 is broken up into 3 accounts with smaller amounts. Those smaller amounts will, in all likelihood, steer you away from the unnecessary purchase. This technique works really well for me.

Always Save a Set Amount

I personally like giving money to my church—always have, always will. I don't consider it a responsibility; I just like the work they do and I consider it necessary. I also adhere to putting a small amount away into savings every month, since it adds up over time.

When I consider a purchase, I try to fight off my impatience. Most of the time I am able to do so, but like everyone else I'm not perfect. The question I always ask myself is, "Can I make this purchase and still save that small monthly amount?" If the answer is "no," then I have to accept the fact that I cannot afford this item at this time. Be patient with your purchases: if you can't fit it into your financial situation right now, it will probably fit in down the road.

In the end, it's not the money that will make you happy: it's what you do with it that will bring value to your life.

In a Nutshell

Money has the potential to be an amazing thing: as it is, it's a required element of life as we know it. It's our choice whether we mistakenly move money up life's list of priorities or keep it in its place as life's least important aspect.

When I teach this principle to an audience, they are initially a bit confused: after all, they are usually in attendance to figure out how to make more money. Although that is true, I am acutely aware that in order for that to occur they must first comprehend that the other aspects of their life, be it spirituality, health, mental wellbeing, or family and friends, all possess more value. If we want money, it must be kept in its place; otherwise, we become out of balance and head for an unfortunate outcome.

By placing a higher value on life's more important aspects, we open up the flow of monetary gain in our direction. I realize it sounds strange for me to say that if you desire more money, then you must make money the least important aspect in your life. But if you do so, it will come to you.

As I have mentioned, I don't make up the success rules: I just teach them. In your heart you know that nothing could be more satisfying than to be in a position to assist someone in their personal financial need. We can start by not being the person saddled with that need!

You either have money or money has you—it's entirely up to you!

Helpful Exercise

I can assure you that there is a really good chance you may have carried some negative views about money into your adult life. These are also known as limiting beliefs. These beliefs mostly reside in our subconscious minds, rendering us unaware that they even exist. Let's counteract some of these limiting beliefs. We can do so by writing a positive statement about the most common ones and look back on them often to internalize them.

Example:

Limiting Belief #1: Money doesn't grow on trees
Proper Viewpoint: Money is in abundance: it is found everywhere.

Limiting Belief #2: They might be rich, but are they happy?
Proper Viewpoint: _____

_____

Limiting Belief #3: Money can't buy friends or happiness
Proper Viewpoint: _____

_____

Limiting Belief #4: Money is the root of all evil
Proper Viewpoint: _____

_____

Limiting Belief #5: What am I, an ATM?

Proper Viewpoint: _____

_____

Money is important but every other aspect of your life is more so!

Too many people spend money they haven't earned, to buy things they don't want, to impress people they don't like.

Will Rogers

FINAL THOUGHTS

I WOULD LIKE to take this opportunity to thank you from my heart for allowing me to use your most valuable resource: your time. I am grateful you have spent it to absorb my thoughts on taking tangible action toward your dreams, goals, and desires.

All of your dreams reside on a path that leads toward your future; it wouldn't be prudent to run full-tilt without regard for your actions. A calculated approach would serve you much better. At the same time, life is short, and the trick is to take into account those solid principles designed to protect you along the way. I did my best to lay out those exact guidelines in this book. I trust you will travel with these principles held close in your heart and mind.

It's time for the awesome life that awaits you. There is nothing that needs to happen in order for you to take that first step. Any other story you make up is just your brain fabricating an untrue reality, enabling its tendency to procrastinate.

Again, thank you for taking the time to ingest my thoughts on this topic; I appreciate it much more than you realize.

God Bless.

It's Time: *Your Awesome Life Awaits.* Yearn for it!

ABOUT THE AUTHOR

ROB LIVES IN Ontario, Canada with Coleen, his wife of 37 years. They split their time between their home in Ajax and a cottage on Belmont Lake. Rob has two amazing children, Josh and Corissa, both of whom are heavily involved in the day-to-day operation of the family business, "Rob Vivian Coaching," one of the largest real estate coaching companies in North America.

Although Rob does draw an immense sense of satisfaction assisting realtors in the accomplishment of their goals, he does find ample time for his three passions: fishing, hockey, and golf.

And, as always, family first!

It's better to fail trying to fly than to sit in the nest and die.

Jentezen Franklin

NOTES